Shields Up

Shields Up

Cybersecurity Project Management

Gregory J. Skulmoski, PhD

BUSINESS EXPERT PRESS
Leader in applied, concise business books

First published in 2022 by
Business Expert Press, LLC
222 East 46th Street, New York, NY 10017
www.businessexpertpress.com

ISBN-13: 978-1-63742-289-2 (paperback)
ISBN-13: 978-1-63742-290-8 (e-book)

Business Expert Press Portfolio and Project Management Collection

First edition: 2022

10 9 8 7 6 5 4 3 2 1

Description

We expect more automation, integration, and online activity in the foreseeable future, resulting in more cybersecurity risks and issues. Therefore, organizations and individuals are spending more resources on cybersecurity projects to implement, maintain, and optimize the confidentiality, integrity, and availability of their digital services and data. The demand for cybersecurity projects and expertise is growing and squeezing the supply of experienced cybersecurity implementers. That is, competent cybersecurity project managers will be progressively in high demand! The result is more cybersecurity technical experts (often in the junior ranks) will be asked to lead their first cybersecurity projects potentially before they are competent to do so; now what?

Shields Up: Cybersecurity Project Management is for our technical friends who are more familiar with Intrusion Detection and Protection Systems (IDPS) than risk registers but are now asked to lead cybersecurity projects. *Shields Up* provides an end-to-end project management framework tuned for cybersecurity projects. More experienced cybersecurity professionals will appreciate the innovative and lean elements of this approach. The reader is guided through the hybrid project management delivery approach and shown essential project management tools that increase the probability of project success.

Cybersecurity project management in *Shields Up* aligns with international standards such as the Guide to the Project Management Body of Knowledge, the National Institute of Standards and Technology Cybersecurity Framework, the ISO 27001 Information Security Management, and ISO 9000 Quality Management. A key feature of *Shields Up* is the reader can quickly apply the hybrid project management approach since it aligns with the global frameworks already followed by cybersecurity subject matter experts (SMEs) leading to more predictable and repeatable projects.

There are *microlearning* and *exercises* sections throughout the book to guide the reader to further learn about cybersecurity project management. Microlearning is an emerging way of continuous professional development where the learner continuously learns in small chunks in addition to attending formal training opportunities like a three-day technology course. The book concludes with Appendixes including career planning tools to help the reader continue their professional development.

Keywords

cybersecurity; hybrid project management; NIST cybersecurity framework; ITIL 4 service management; Lean Six Sigma Optimization; risk management; certified information systems security professional; CISSP; continuous improvement; digital transformation; agile; career planning; lean management

Contents

Testimonials

Shields Up was reviewed by a heterogeneous group of diverse experts in technology, cybersecurity, and project management. The project management reviewers include both researchers and thought leaders in the project management specialty not only with decades of experience but also practicing as technology project managers. The cybersecurity reviewers are not typical book reviewers (e.g., academics); instead, these reviewers work in cybersecurity and related technical domains, resulting in a practical understanding of project management and cybersecurity. Therefore, these technology innovators know exactly the challenges and demands of cybersecurity projects and are well-placed to provide critical reviews such as the following:

"Must Read"

"Shields Up: Cybersecurity Project Management *is comprehensive and incredibly timely, given the ever-increasing cybersecurity threat landscape. It should be a must-read for all IT project managers because of the importance of ensuring that all IT projects clearly and deliberately address cyber risks as just a normal part of the process. You stated it perfectly when you wrote, 'It is good practice to build cybersecurity into our projects rather than adding cybersecurity as the project prepares to go-live.' The most important takeaway is the multitude of methodologies and frameworks that IT professionals look to for guidance can be nicely aligned and integrated into a coherent delivery model without compromising quality or efficiency. I must commend Greg on a well-written and comprehensive guide for tackling this new digital world we live in. Well done!"*—**Jason Roos, Chief Information Officer, King Abdullah University of Science and Technology, Saudi Arabia**

"Perfect Alignment"

"*The book* Shields Up: Cybersecurity Project Management *covers a broad spectrum of a reader's possible role within an IT department, especially in managing strategic and operational projects, including cybersecurity. The book will be appreciated by those who perform roles like project management, quality management, risk management, cybersecurity, IT operations support, strategic planning, and more. I was surprised to see its perfect alignment with NIST, ITIL, PMBOK® Guide, even ISO Risk Management. I advocate for a risk-based approach to managing cybersecurity, a central theme in* Shields Up. *This book shares essential knowledge and expertise, and Greg nailed these and many more."*—**Irene Corpuz, PMP, ITIL, CISA, CEH, ISO 27001, Lead Implementer and Auditor, Manager—Projects, Federal Higher Education, United Arab Emirates**

"Outstanding Project Management Practice"

"Dr. Skulmoski's book is a metaphor for outstanding project management practice. It delivers content that's critical for the fast-developing business climate, and it does so with a precision of timeliness that is commendable. Shields Up *will prepare project managers to successfully deliver technology and cybersecurity projects."*—**Professor Alan Patching, PhD, Project Management, Associate Dean External Engagement, Bond University, Australia**

"Clearly and Succinctly Guides Cybersecurity Professionals"

"In Shields Up, *Skulmoski clearly and succinctly guides cybersecurity professionals on how to incorporate project management techniques and principles into their work to enhance both their projects and careers. He is clearly in tune with the struggles of cybersecurity professionals and the significant demands on their time. By providing expert advice on managing projects, which includes the latest thoughts and developments in the field, he gives cybersecurity professionals the critical tools they'll need to be successful."*—**Derek Molnar, PMP, IT Project Manager, Colorado State University, United States**

"A Solid Guide"

*"*Shields Up *is a solid guide covering all the stages and standards commonly found in cybersecurity projects, future demands, and a deep dive into why the IT delivery gap will only worsen due to skills shortage and increased demand for projects. The book perfectly covers standards, measurement practices (KPIs/ SLAs), and guiding principles around cybersecurity project management from an end-to-end project perspective. Overall, the book richly describes the*

whole picture around technical project management at an enjoyable and great pace."—**Thiago Santos, Senior Technical Architect, Mulesoft, Canada**

"Pragmatic, Informative, and an Enjoyable Read"

"I begin by giving kudos to the author for writing this book. I found it very pragmatic, informative, and an enjoyable read. Shields *Up is well-structured and easy to read. The author provides a solid introduction to the cybersecurity and project management specialties supplemented with exercises and microlearning opportunities. Additionally, I found the illustrations very helpful as they summarize the knowledge and aids learning retention, especially for each guiding framework (e.g., NIST, ITIL 4, and PMBOK® Guide).*

The book has the right balance between technical and project management content and is well suited for cybersecurity professionals and most technical roles. Shields Up *will also appeal to those who work in project management offices (PMOs).*

A vital benefit of this book is it can guide technical professionals to transition to a project management career. This book can be a quick reference guide to bridge the knowledge gap between technical and project management areas of practice. Overall, I enjoyed reading Shields Up *and recommend it to technical professionals interested in advancing their careers."*—**Israa Abulawi, BEng, ISACA, Enterprise Project Manager, Healthcare Care Technology and Data Management, United Arab Emirates**

"Unique Resource"

*"*Shields Up *is a truly unique resource. It explores the important domain of cybersecurity through a project management lens. I have not seen a book like this that is so comprehensive in scope and rich in advice while also being extremely practical. I believe this is mandatory reading for anyone wanting to make a career in our increasingly digital world of business transformation."*—**Professor Craig Langston, PhD, Project Management, Bond University, Australia**

Foreword

It was late July of 2012, and I had just landed in Abu Dhabi, having accepted a role with IBM in Middle East and Africa. I had been hired to set up and execute the learning function for a greenfield digital hospital, Cleveland Clinic Abu Dhabi. Recruited into IBM on the basis of my success implementing training programs for clinicians, I arrived at the temporary offices of Cleveland Clinic my first day of work sweating and jet-lagged, and met my key client, Dr. Gregory Skulmoski.

Greg was keen and cheerful, impeccably dressed, and energetic with a spring in his step. He greeted me enthusiastically. Though I already possessed almost 15 years of IT project management experience at that point, the subsequent weeks, months, and years working alongside Greg were an education. Some of my new colleagues loathed submitting deliverables (e.g., detailed requirements) to Greg as his reviews were exhaustive. Indeed, Greg insisted on the highest levels of quality, and in his exigence demonstrated deep familiarity with the theory and practice of project management.

I later learned that Greg's focus on quality assurance (preventing mistakes) rather than on quality control (fixing defects) was a team-building effort where the goal was to reinforce the *attention to details* skill and to get the technology right the first time, a very lean approach. Greg's teams delivered all their projects on time, and the go-live monitoring phase was exceptionally quiet indicating successful technology adoption. Greg's projects were closed out early because the new technology was predictable, reliable, and fit-for-purpose: technology characteristics that bring confidence to end users. When the project finished, vendors were able to cleanly depart because poor quality was never an issue; I appreciate that Greg took care of his vendors too.

Dr. Skulmoski also proved himself well-equipped and conversant in adult learning and training theory (andragogy), program and subject learning outcomes, instructional design, and many other components required for successful learning. Forward to March 2015, and we opened the doors of Cleveland Clinic Abu Dhabi on time, and all caregivers could use the best-in-class systems to provide compassionate care. Greg would go on to accept a professorship at Bond University after a few years, and I subsequently carried forward what I learned working with Greg into a dozen other contexts in four countries, experimenting, relearning, yet much of the time standing on a foundation of certainties forged during my time working alongside Greg.

Throughout all these engagements I have participated in since leaving the site of Cleveland Clinic Abu Dhabi, several themes continue to emerge: How can project teams simultaneously combine the best of Agile and waterfall delivery methods? How can organizations address the "skills gap" in mission-critical fields such as cybersecurity? And how can large groups of clients and vendors come together to achieve results quickly and amicably?

In *Shields Up: Cybersecurity Project Management*, Greg artfully and scientifically cuts a path through the thicket of the contemporary project landscape, offering full-featured roadmaps to guide all those who might struggle with modern project management. But his treatment is more wide-ranging than just these areas. His framing and analyses of the current problems in business partner expectations, the pace of technological change, and the increasing importance of cybersecurity are all rock solid and extensively researched. He has also taken great care to engage his readers by creating exercises that will help them adapt their reading of this book and apply it to the cybersecurity project management conundrums they face today.

Shields Up is well-balanced, including meaningfully deep summaries of waterfall, Agile, and lean project management approaches, while keeping a pace crisp enough to prevent you from ever putting the book down. I found myself drawn to continue reading. Greg includes just the right amount of detail but includes numerous useful references, making it a suitable guide without ever becoming heavy reading.

Hybrid project management is a must-have ability in today's business environment, and Greg has elegantly detailed a flexible approach to mixing and matching the best of predictive and adaptive project management disciplines and allowing the reader to match techniques to suit the context of their own cybersecurity project.

For seasoned professionals in project management, *Shields Up* offers exceptionally clear and succinct explanations of critically important practices such as project initiation document structure, three-point estimation, risk and issue framework, and quality management. I found myself going back to review the text several times, capturing notes and slides, and then immediately putting many of Greg's hybrid project management practices into play in my latest project!

As you will observe in your reading of this work, *Shields Up* is lightweight and eminently practical. I find the approach refreshing and uplifting in its directness and simplicity. Like an authentically prepared "sugo" or a properly performed press-up, many of the fundamentals of project management are superficially understood by many yet poorly executed by most. Getting them right, while elusive, can mean obtaining extraordinarily results. In this book, Dr. Gregory Skulmoski presents you with tangible and effective methods to produce extraordinary results in your cybersecurity projects.

—Chris Walker, SHRM-SCP

Preface

Digital business transformation and emerging cyber-physical systems create unprecedented security risk

—Gartner 2020a, 1

Shields Up: Cybersecurity Project Management meets the demand for cybersecurity professionals to develop project management competencies to lead and succeed in their cybersecurity projects. Technology adoption and pervasiveness are increasing and perhaps accelerating, driven by Fourth Industrial Revolution innovations, and Covid-19 triggered digital transformation projects. *Shields Up* is designed to provide cybersecurity and other technology professionals a guide to plan, develop, manage, and implement cybersecurity projects.

Shields Up is divided into two parts: (i) Rising Demand for Technology and Cybersecurity and (ii) Hybrid Project Management. Part 1 frames project management in the context of an innovation delivery method; that is, to achieve strategic objectives, organizations increasingly initiate projects. The technology forecast is an increased demand for technology and cybersecurity. What is driving the demand for technology? What is the future foresight (examining possible future scenarios)?

Part 1: Increasing Demand for Cybersecurity Projects

Organizations that are agile and responsive to changing expectations and fleeting opportunities look to technology to gain a competitive advantage. They may implement technology to deliver new products and services or make processes more efficient by removing waste. By making processes lean and reducing materials or the time in the process, organizations attempt to satisfy customers. Satisfied customers purchase goods and services and make repeat purchases. Therefore, optimization and digitization are common business goals. Organizations also collaborate and connect people, systems, and data with technology; we see hyperconnectivity increasing and extended digital ecosystems forming. Once digital trans-formation projects are implemented, organizations desire analytics-based decision-making capabilities; more technology projects with shortened delivery expectations are done right the first time!

In response to the increased demand for technology, organizations also see amplified demand for cybersecurity services ranging from pro-tecting data assets to adding the new technology to the organization's threat monitoring systems. Business partners become collaborators in innovation, value cybersecurity services, and support increased cyberse-curity budgets to secure their technology-driven innovations. However, with larger cybersecurity budgets, IT leadership is held accountable to meet business expectations. An issue facing the profession is a severe cybersecurity skills gap; organizations struggle to meet the demand for cybersecurity services due to a shortage of qualified cybersecurity pro-fessionals, including project managers. Many organizations have unfilled cybersecurity positions with long recruitment times. A consequence of these dynamics is cybersecurity professionals are asked to lead routine cybersecurity projects, leaving more complex cybersecurity projects for experienced project managers.

Organizations not only face challenges of implementing and managing more technologies, keeping systems and information secure, and complet-ing work despite unfilled cybersecurity positions, they may also see more cybersecurity regulation. Governments and regulatory bodies are intro-ducing cybersecurity regulations, and some organization are obligated to comply. Cybersecurity maturity models provide a pathway and guidance toward compliance and maturity targets, such as the Cybersecurity Capa-bility Maturity Model (C2M2). Cybersecurity regulatory compliance drives more cybersecurity projects such as internal and external audits.

Organizations leverage cybersecurity and related standards and frame-works to fulfill cybersecurity expectations and requirements. There are two prominent cybersecurity standards to guide organizations to opti-mize their services: the Framework for Improving Critical Infrastructure Cybersecurity by the National Institute of Standards and Technology (NIST) and ISO 27001 Information Security Management (National Institute of Standards and Technology 2018, 1–55). IT departments may follow the Infrastructure Technology Information Library (ITIL) standard to meet the demand for a service or product through planning, designing, developing, testing, implementing, operating, and optimizing phases to deliver value to the end user. While project management is explicitly embedded in ITIL, project management standards guide delivering value through a continuum of delivery approaches ranging from the predictive traditional (waterfall) project management delivery approach to adaptive agile techniques like Scrum and Kanban. The Guide to the Project Management Body of Knowledge (PMBOK® Guide) and PRINCE2 are two prominent project management standards supported with professional certifications. Central to cybersecurity, ITIL service management, and project management is quality management and the ISO 9001 quality management standard that guides organizations along a continuous improvement path.

Technology adoption is increasing at an accelerated rate due to many drivers such as artificial intelligence, the cloud, sensors, IoT devices, and the promise of technology-driven innovation. More technology results in increased demand for cybersecurity services. More regulation results in an increased demand for cybersecurity services. Increased demand translates into an increase in cybersecurity projects in an environment with a shortage of cybersecurity professionals and project managers. And hence, the purpose of *Shields Up: Cybersecurity Project Management* is to provide a proven method to plan, manage, and deliver cybersecurity projects aligned with leading global standards and best practices.

Part 2: Hybrid Project Management

The hybrid project management method is based on the traditional project management approach (predictive) with iterations where required. Hybrid project management draws on principles from the Agile Manifesto, the PMBOK® Guide, and other standards and frameworks. The project manager tailors principles, processes, tools, and methods suitable for the organization, project, and task. Tailoring can provide a lean project management delivery approach that facilitates the team being able to focus on producing products and services.

Most cybersecurity projects can be delivered with the traditional project management approach (initiate, plan, design, build, test, implement, monitor/stabilize, and closeout) and traditional project management processes (e.g., quality and risk management). Hybrid project management utilizes traditional project management methods like scheduling, budgeting, and managing change. Innovative techniques are included in *Shields Up*, like Perfect-Likely-Outrageous (PLO, see *Project Schedule*) estimating and assessing your cybersecurity project with the Project Management Gizmo to develop a deep understanding of the project. Each cybersecurity project phase is tuned, a lean project management approach is described, and the processes, tools, and considerations are outlined.

Unfortunately, project failure is far too common in technology and cybersecurity projects. Project planning and risk management can improve the probability of project success. *Shields Up* outlines a lean planning process to deliver a project plan ready to take into the approval process. Even the best project plans can fail if risk management is poorly executed. Therefore, with quality management, risk management is at the heart of hybrid project management. Risk management need not be complicated with charts and statistical analyses; an intuitive qualitative risk management method often underlies successfully managing cybersecurity projects.

Supplemental material is included in *Shields Up* appendixes to take your learning further. The Project Management Gizmo tool helps assess your cybersecurity project and is included with permission from the International Project Management Association, presented in Rome, 2008. Any project can be assessed with the Gizmo to develop a comprehensive understanding of the project to begin the planning phase. When the Gizmo is used by the project manager, project sponsor, and team, a shared understanding of the project develops, and the probability of success improves.

A second appendix guides the reader to complete an iteration of career planning timed to coincide with an annual performance review. We are guided by best practices to continually improve not only systems but also our human resources. We also have a cybersecurity skills shortage. Therefore, the cybersecurity professional is encouraged to undertake career planning. *Shields Up* guides the reader through career planning steps to achieve career goals and build a sustainable career.

Finally, throughout the book, there are supplemental exercises and further guidance. *Shields Up* provides an approach to planning, managing, and delivering cybersecurity projects. The tools and practices can immediately be applied to your projects, and the exercises guide you to apply *Shields Up*. Many of the concepts outlined in this book can be supplemented with readily available online materials to extend your understanding of project management principles and theory. *Shields Up* provides microlearning opportunities in each chapter for the reader to increase their hybrid project management competence and success in projects.

Learning Outcomes

This book aims to provide an upskilling pathway for those interested in deepening their understanding of cybersecurity project management.[1] There are three learning outcomes for this book.

1. Apply hybrid project management to the increasing demand for more cybersecurity projects requiring formal project management competencies.
2. Implement cybersecurity project management aligned with global IT frameworks like NIST and ITIL.
3. Acquire and use hybrid project management principles and skills.

By reading this book and using it to plan and implement cybersecurity projects, the learner will better understand project management in the context of cybersecurity management and ultimately deliver successful cybersecurity projects.

---

[1] While *Shields Up* is focused on cybersecurity projects, the hybrid project management approach, processes and tools, can be applied to most technology and innovation projects such as automation, integration, and robotics projects.

Acknowledgments

I worked in Finance crunching numbers and one day my boss asked me to purchase twelve 386 CPU computers as part of the annual capital budgeting cycle: my first "IT project." Later, I participated in the selection team for a new financial system. We implemented a customized system that was late and over budget. I wanted to learn more about business to become better at projects, and I completed a traditional MBA. Even with this new business knowledge about labor law, return on investment calculations, and the four pillars of marketing, my projects continued to struggle. I searched for answers and discovered the project management specialty.

I enrolled in a project management program at the University of Calgary and learned how to plan and implement projects. I had many teachers who taught me the tools, processes, and finer points about project management. Thank you, professors Francis Hartman, George Jergeas, Janice Thomas, and Mr. Ken Hanley. All had practical project experience and helped me develop my own approach to managing projects. Dr. Francis Hartman led the project management specialization program and brought together engaged students to learn and have fun while polishing their assignments. Very quickly it seems that I almost finished my dissertation and thinking about what to do next? I spoke with Francis, and he recommended the Middle East. Shortly thereafter, I was hired by Zayed University in Abu Dhabi, United Arab Emirates, to teach project management.

I taught project management in the College of Information Technology for nine years and enjoyed academia and see our students learn and graduate. However, I yearned to practice what I professed; to manage my own projects. I joined Cleveland Clinic Abu Dhabi as a project manager near the beginning of the project and delivered 14 strategic projects ranging from technical (e.g., IoT/cloud technologies) to nontechnical projects (e.g., internal auditing). I worked in a PMO that followed leading standards such as ITIL, ISO 27000, ISO 9001, and the PMBOK®

Guide (more about these in Part 1). I experienced how multiple standards and frameworks can coexist to support delivering projects on time, on budget, and to the right levels of quality. I learned from my leadership (both technical and clinical), and I am grateful for the collegiality of my colleagues and team members. The tools, processes, and techniques in *Shields Up* were implemented and refined delivering projects at Cleveland Clinic Abu Dhabi. I was fortunate to win the 2017 Middle East Security Award, Chief Information Security Officers Council—*100 Rising Stars in Security and Risk* for how I managed risks in technology projects: hybrid project management works. After seven years of being on the sharp end of projects, I returned to academia and joined the project management program at Bond University, Australia.

I enjoyed being back in the classroom with diverse project experiences to share with our students. I joined a robust project management program with active and impactful researchers. My colleague Dr. Amir Ghanbaripour reviewed *Shields Up* and commented on the people aspect of projects: "The people who carry the shields are far more important than the shields (technology) themselves when it comes to cybersecurity." My students are also a source of influence: they graduate, work, and often contact me with their own stories of successfully applying the techniques in *Shields Up*. During this time, Dr. Kam Jugdev contacted me about writing a project management book for the Business Experts Press (BEP). We were PhD students at the University of Calgary and had previously published together. I teach a technology project management subject that includes unique content appearing in *Shields Up*. I am grateful to Dr. Jugdev and the BEP Collection Editor: Dr. Timothy Kloppenborg for their guidance. The BEP publications and Exeter Premedia Services team were skilled professionals who live and breathe lean project management to efficiently bring *Shields Up* to life. Thank you.

PART I

Increasing Demand for Cybersecurity

CHAPTER 1

Introduction

We live in extraordinary times; technological advances make headlines daily like "In the next decade, we'll experience more progress than in the last 100 years combined, as technology reshapes health and materials sciences, energy, transportation, and a wide range of other industries and domains" (Corbo and Ostojic 2021, 2). These technology promises are tempered with cyber-doom headlines like "Age of the cyber-attack: the US struggles to curb the rise of digital destabilization" (Rushe and Borger 2021, 1). To enjoy the benefits of transformative technologies, we need to keep these technologies and data safe to use. More technological adoption results in more cybersecurity projects. A project is "a temporary endeavor undertaken to create a unique product, service, or result. The temporary nature of projects indicates a beginning and an end to the project work or a phase of the project work" (PMI 2021, 28). Some organizations complete work through "initiatives" that are miniprojects with less complexity and risk (e.g., install an application patch). Technology professionals implementing initiatives can benefit from hybrid project management practices and tailoring; however, the focus in *Shields Up* is on more extensive and complex projects where project success is not easily guaranteed. But first, let's differentiate between projects and operations.

Projects Versus Operations

Information technology (IT) departments provide IT services like e-mail and business applications that cybersecurity teams keep safe and secure. End users leverage these services to complete their work to benefit their customers and organization; this is business operations. Service gaps and continuous improvement opportunities are identified, prioritized, and implemented as projects during business operations. Thus, projects feed into operations to help the business achieve its strategic objectives

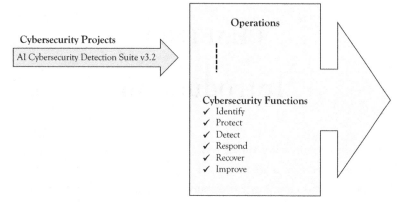

Figure 1.1 Projects deliver value to operations

(Figure 1.1). For example, IT provides cybersecurity services behind the scenes for most in the organization but are considered operations since we provide these services every day. We may encounter a problem that we need to rectify or identify an opportunity we wish to leverage; either can trigger a request for a new project. In Figure 1.1, we see that IT has identified an opportunity to improve threat detection functionality; they have approved and initiated a project to implement new detection software. By the length of the arrow, the project team is close to delivering the software into operations. We also notice the vertical dashed line in operations signifying a monitoring period after go live to fix any defects and optimize the new service.

We also implement projects for our business partners, such as upgrading our Enterprise Resource Planning (ERP) system or company website. Thus, we have operations and projects; we meet the needs of our stakeholders by initiating and delivering value into operations through projects. We follow the project management life cycle to deliver new IT services. Delivering new technical services using project management contributes to achieving business strategy (George 2008, 1).

The business initiates new projects for many reasons, such as responding to threats or vulnerabilities, taking advantage of an opportunity, increasing revenues, decreasing costs, or regulatory compliance, as we have seen. Typically, a new project request is sent to an entity with approval

Figure 1.2 Change authorization board

authority like a change authorization board (Figure 1.2). A business case accompanies the request, and the proposed service and project is evaluated. The new project request may be approved, rejected, put on hold for future consideration, or require further information upon which a decision will be made. Some cybersecurity projects may be initiated through a formal committee, while others will be approved within the IT department. In Figure 1.2, the change authorization board has approved an internal cybersecurity audit to prepare for accreditation by an external agency.

Going through a formal change control process adds value for the organization:

1. Allow prioritization of requests for new IT services.
2. Contribute to meeting regulatory requirements.
3. Reduce the number of failed projects.
4. Better manage the flow of projects through the organization.
5. Improve our understanding of quality, time, scope, and time requirements for the project.
6. Provide a forum for businesses to propose new projects and services.

Some of the projects you will be asked to lead may come through a project prioritization and control process. We see organizations increasingly implementing more technology and cybersecurity projects using change authorization boards.

Technology Forecast: Change, Change, and More Projects

Working in the IT field, we see constant technological change. I am reminded that "change is certain in everything except vending machines"; soon, vending machines will become digital payment only. The changes underway are detailed in the *Fourth Industrial Revolution: World Economic Forum* where the researchers describe the Fourth Industrial Revolution as a digital revolution fusing digital, biological, and physical entities (Schwab 2016, 7). A distinguishing characteristic is the exponential speed at which these technologies emerge, bringing significant impact: "The scale of the impact and the speed of the changes taking place have made the transformation that is playing out so different from any other industrial revolution in human history" (Schwab 2016, 109). Data processing and communications are proceeding at ever-accelerating speed, which stresses data volumes, storage capacity, processing, and knowledge created (Creese, Saunders, Axon, and Dixon 2020, 10) and can trigger new projects (e.g., upgrade the infrastructure). We see some organizations embracing a continuous flow of digital transformation projects (Creese et al. 2020, 10), as seen in overall increases in IT budgets (Columbus 2020, 1).

We see people connecting with mobile technologies with unprecedented computing power, storage capacity, and functionality to access broad knowledge databases. Transformational technologies are emerging like artificial intelligence (AI), data modeling, 3D printing, nanomanufacturing, quantum computing, large-scale energy storage, and so forth. The popular literature trumpets the new age of digital acceleration and change (Table 1.1).

Our managers read these articles from digital thought leaders, expecting continued and accelerated technological advances. These bring digital opportunities to leverage and vulnerabilities to secure. These influential reports now drive business strategy, and new technologies change our customer expectations. These emerging technological promises are often translated into requests for new projects and secure systems. More cybersecurity projects are coming our way!

Table 1.1 Digital acceleration and change

Source	Message	Comment
McHugh (2020, 1)	"The pace of automation is accelerating, with more organizations creating fully automated value chains"	Now I have to worry about keeping our systems secure and the security of our partners' systems
Mulesoft (2020, 4)	"Organizations are increasingly investing in AI capabilities to expedite and personalize customer service, reduce human bias, and increase productivity"	These business requirements sound good, but that is a lot of technology to be secured!
Blackburn, LaBerge, O'Toole, and Schneider (2020, 3)	"Bold, tightly integrated digital strategies are the most effective approach to digital transformation"	Bold! I'm already working overtime to keep our data and systems safe and secure
Gonzalo, Harreis, Altable, and Villepelet (2020, 5)	"Companies must accelerate their online capabilities in both demand generation and operations management"	Accelerate? I already stated I am working overtime!
Skilton and Hovsepian (2018, 60)	"The near to longer-term impact of artificial intelligence and the fusion of intelligent systems into industries, individuals, and societies will have a profound impact on the role of the human at work and human experience"	I knew this 10 years ago! I live the profound impact systems have every day!
PMI (2018, 6)	A PMI report found 85% of the jobs that will be available by 2030 haven't even been invented yet!	I can barely keep current technologies safe, let alone technologies required to support jobs that don't yet exist
Scheibenreif and Raskino (2021, 1)	"Machine customers represent the biggest new growth opportunity of the decade. In fact, by 2030, at least 25% of all purchasing decisions will be delegated to machines"	Now, I need to think about machines being hacked, resulting in machine customers illegally using our credit cards!

Disruptive Technologies Acceleration

Innovation and technology adoption is accelerating, and there is a feeling that if organizations do not implement a digital transformation strategy, it may be too late for laggards to catch up to technology early adopters (Aaldering and Song 2021, 12). Indeed, Covid-19 triggered a massive acceleration of digitization (Scholtz 2021, 2). These technologies need to be secured as they can present new vulnerabilities. However, as the pace of technology adoption accelerates, so will the need to secure technologies also accelerate. Thus, early adopters will likely continue to implement technology at an accelerated pace, and laggards will try to catch up. The result will be more technology projects and more cybersecurity work at an accelerated cadence.

New Technologies to Protect

The specific technologies and trends are less important here; the general trends related to technology adoption are of greater interest. We see the rollout of 5G technologies leading to a new era of connectivity, complexity, and opportunity for organizations and bad actors. The World Economic Forum (Creese et al. 2020, 6) predicts the following transformative technologies will be increasingly important: ubiquitous connectivity, AI and machine learning, quantum computing and next-generation identify, and access management. Combining technologies like IoT and sensors will bring new opportunities and assets to protect. Organizations will increasingly move components of their technology ecosystem to the cloud, thereby adding additional complexity to cybersecurity efforts.

We can expect transformative change with next-generation computing like computational collaboration, distributed computing, and quantum computing resulting in increased computing speed and efficiency. Early adopters will have a disruptive advantage and can transform strategy, operations, supply chains, and markets (Corbo and Ostojic 2021, 2). It is no surprise that our organizations have early adopters who will propose new technologies to help us innovate. Expect more proposals that include AI technologies. However, these emerging technologies change the risk equation with increased and evolving threats, widening attacks, continued structural weaknesses, and grave consequences due to cyberattacks (Creese et al. 2020, 13).

AI Technologies Become Mainstream

AI is the next big thing (PMI 2019, 2). We see AI early adopters in several industries, including advertising, automotive, banking, electronics, financial services, health care, insurance, media, pharmaceuticals, telecommunications, and transportation (Corbo and Ostojic 2021, 2). We can expect AI to be widely applied to:

1. Automation and productivity improvements across the value chain;
2. Next-generation customer experience;
3. Transformation in research and product development;
4. New business models, products, and services (Corbo and Ostojic 2021, 2).

Therefore, we will see more AI-related projects implementing applied AI applications and services. These AI-supported applications and services will need cybersecurity involvement.

We can expect the emergence of IoT to grow and accelerate as equipment vendors stay connected to their devices in the field to predict maintenance requirements using AI (Dahlqvist, Patel, Rajko, and Shulman 2019, 3). The technological advances in sensor technologies and the adoption of smart cities are also driving IoT adoption (Dahlqvist et al. 2019, 3). We may see nano IoT sensors attached to the human body, ingested, or integrated with organs to allow human body monitoring and augmentation (Skilton and Hovsepian 2018, 30). Innovations like ingested IoT sensors are examples of the rapidly growing IoT technology segment. Indeed, we may see as many as 50 billion IoT devices by 2022, and such "rapid proliferation has made these products appealing targets for a growing number of cyberattacks" (Microsoft 2020, 30). Again, there are more opportunities for cybersecurity services delivered through projects.

Unfortunately, bad actors will increasingly use AI and associated technologies in their cyberattacks. For example, the malicious use of AI will become more sophisticated and pervasive, where automating attacks can see increases to attack speed and scale (Creese et al. 2020, 28). Adversarial machine learning (actions to attack machine learning) is predicted to grow (Microsoft 2020, 35). The attackers will be able to extract more value from stolen data and will be able to deliver more damage from their attacks (Creese et al. 2020, 12). Offensive AI will find new ways of attacking its targets. AI defenses will also see an increase in adoption by organizations and individuals. AI defense capabilities will see an improving defense posture, dynamic threat detection, proactive defense, increased speed in response and recovery, and improvements to attack determination (Creese et al. 2020, 29). AI will help us detect threats in languages we do not understand and find and understand malicious patterns that no human would ever consider (CyberEdge Group, LLC 2020, 34). "We might even go out on a limb and say that machine learning and other AI technologies offer our last chance to catch up with and overtake the bad guys" (CyberEdge Group, LLC 2020, 35). More cybersecurity projects are predicted.

CHAPTER 2

Customer's Expectations Driving IT Departments

We see emerging trends that impact the nature of projects and are driven by our customers (internal and external), resulting in an expansion of IT services delivered through projects; these services require cybersecurity. Organizations invest in digital transformation projects for quick wins, high feasibility/high-value potential projects, and "moonshot" projects with a high return on investment but low feasibility (Obwegeser, Yokoi, Wade, and Voskes 2020, 8). Business is increasingly partnering with IT to implement projects that will transform their business. What do our customers expect from IT?

Quest for More Agility

Customers desire flexibility and speed to respond to new opportunities; they desire agility.[1] They need scalable systems (Barquin, Dreischmeier, Hertli, Königsfeld, and Roth 2020, 2) and support for business changes. Indeed, we will see more combining technologies (e.g., sensors and IoT) through integration to deliver new business value (Corbo and Ostojic 2021, 2). Thus, our business partners increasingly see technology as a solution to problems and a way to quickly leverage innovation opportunities (business agility).

---

[1] Business agility is different than traditional agile project management, which uses the Scrum delivery method with the Agile Manifesto as its foundation. Business agility is about the ability to continuously deliver value by quickly leveraging market opportunities in a turbulent environment.

Pursue Innovation

Today, we hear "disrupt or be disrupted" as a call for innovation; whether incremental improvement or large-scale transformation, organizations are pursuing digital transformation through technical projects (PMI 2020, 2). Business leaders read that "most companies will need to build new digital businesses to stay economically viable" (Williams, Galvin, and LaBerge 2021, 3). Indeed, some recommend a proactive innovation mindset to succeed in the emerging hypercompetitive environment (PMI 2020, 5). Early adopters of emerging technologies will most likely reap the most benefits (Corbo and Ostojic 2021, 15). Some of the most common digital transformation projects include digitizing the end-user experience, scaling, and enhancing the organization's infrastructure (Dhasarathy, Gill, and Khan 2020, 2). Thus, cybersecurity professionals have the unique opportunity to ensure that the benefits promised by technological innovations can be delivered.

Optimize Lean Operations

The quest toward lean operations is a business strategy to do more with less; it delivers products and services efficiently and effectively. Achieving lean operations positions the unit or organization to be more competitive. Lean advocates strive to reduce steps in processes to make the process more efficient and remove "pain points." We also try to reduce waste in materials and human resources used in the process. The Lean Six Sigma approach is a problem-solving technique to identify opportunities for improvement, often followed up with a process-improvement project. Many process-improvement projects have technology, integration, and automation at their core. These digital transformation activities can increase cybersecurity vulnerabilities for some organizations (Boehm et al. 2021, 8). Pandemic-driven digital transformation contributed to additional vulnerabilities due to the rapid implementation pace (Williams et al. 2021, 5). The desire to become leaner through technology can require more cybersecurity efforts and projects to address companion cybersecurity vulnerabilities.

What Is Microlearning?

Traditional training involves attending a training course for a few days. After a few months, the learning decays unless it is refreshed or used. With microlearning, learner continuously acquires new knowledge that can be applied to real work. The duration for microlearning is often only a few minutes each day to read an article at the time of their choosing (Bleich 2021, 2). Microlearning can be more effective when the learner follows a learning to do list (Bersin and Zao-Sanders 2019, 2).

Microlearning

The following topics can improve your understanding and application of lean management principles and methods.

- Think about lean-oriented projects in your organization; what are the project sponsor's goals? Reduce time through the process? Automate manual steps? Reduce costs? Understanding the high-level request will help to understand detailed requirements.
- Learn about Lean Six Sigma as a process-improvement technique.

Digitize End-User Experiences

Business is reimagining the role of technology with a greater focus on leveraging technology to achieve and report upon business objectives (Dhasarathy et al. 2020, 2). We will continue to see requests for projects to transition from manual to automated processes and interactions (Dhasarathy et al. 2020, 2). The digitization of manual processes may be an output from a Lean Six Sigma or quality-improvement study to identify process optimization opportunities. Unfortunately, we see that "risk management has not kept pace with the proliferation of digital and analytics transformations" (Boehm and Smith 2021, 2); we may have been prioritizing on-time and on-budget delivery targets at the expense of optimized cybersecurity.

Improve Processes With Automation

We see the drive toward leanness and digitization to accelerate the demand for automation projects. CIOs (Chief Information Officer) are invited to partner with the business to deliver "high impact initiatives" (Gartner 2020b, 3). There is a growing imperative for automation projects to reduce costs through reduced human involvement and improvements to customer experience. Automation and robotics will be a growth area since a diverse suite of technologies (e.g., IoT, AI, sensors, and machine intelligence) will be combined to create new automation opportunities (Skilton and Hovespian 2018, 59). Again, we will see more automation and integration projects requiring cybersecurity.

Enable Hyperconnectivity

Organizations are racing to connect with partners and applications (Mulesoft 2021, 4) and external data to improve competitiveness (Aaser and McElhaney 2021, 2). More connections can bring additional innovation and opportunities; increased connectivity can potentially bring more cybersecurity vulnerabilities. The nature of connections is also evolving with complex systems relationships forming among the physical, biological, and digital domains (Skilton and Hovsepian 2018, 55). More connections lead to digital ecosystems development. However, hyperconnected environments present the problem where an attack on the digital ecosystem can negatively impact downstream actors dependent on the attacked asset (Creese et al. 2020, 21).

Join the Emerging Digital Ecosystem

Business initiatives strive to connect an organization's systems; however, they also desire more connections with external partners and customers. Digital ecosystems are emerging that integrate business-to-business and business-to-consumer interactions (Dietz, Khan, and Rab 2020, 3) to create value for all stakeholders in the network (Diana and Torrance 2020, 1). We can expect businesses to request more participation in digital ecosystems to keep up with fast-evolving customers and workers

(Dhasarathy et al. 2020, 2). These ecosystems are complex and welcomed by consumers; however, they present the potential for additional vulnerabilities to be managed by the cybersecurity teams.

> To repeat, organizations are focused on delivering value; therefore, tuning our technical ecosystems and processes to optimize value aligns business and IT goals.

Meet Shorter Delivery Expectations

Organizations are maturing with their project management and are beginning to measure key performance indicators (KPIs) for how quickly projects are initiated, planned, designed, built, tested, and delivered to the end-user (Fitzpatrick and Strovink 2021, 4). There is a shift from failing quickly to succeeding quickly in projects (PMI 2020, 2). One of the early issues related to speedy delivery cycles is that cybersecurity might not receive sufficient treatment resulting in avoidable vulnerabilities (Boehm and Smith 2021, 2).

Provide Analytics-Based Decision Making

Digital transformation projects are changing how we work. As our digital connections increase and processes are optimized, the business will be data thirsty when faced with decisions. We see an increased demand for analytics as a vehicle to provide the organization with a competitive advantage (Dietz et al. 2020, 6). Expect more AI-supported analytics with data inputs from a wide variety of sources. One result of using AI-supported analytics is that businesses will predict new opportunities that may become new projects to implement and more digital services to protect. Indeed, analytics-based decision making is at the core of cybersecurity best practices.

Conclusion of Customer Expectations

It is no surprise that technology demand and adoption are increasing and quickly. The demand is multidimensional, beginning with the desire to drive down costs and increase value for an organization's customers through optimization and transformation projects (Moyer 2021, 3). Organizations are forging ahead with digital transformation and innovation projects, requiring new technology to improve competitiveness. Technology is leveraged to connect with business partners and customers in an ever-evolving digital ecosystem. Our purpose is to protect those systems and data. Therefore, as we see more demand for digital services, we will also see more demand for cybersecurity services; the attack canvas is becoming more sophisticated (Skilton and Hovsepian 2018, 36). Indeed, due to regulation and insurance requirements, we may see more cybersecurity compliance projects. Thus, more technology projects bring more cybersecurity project work with the expectation that the project will be done the first time and delivered on time and on budget.

CHAPTER 3

Future of Cybersecurity

We know that the reach and pace of digital transformation are increasing and accelerating. More technology equates to more cybersecurity work. The cloud, AI, IoT, and emerging technologies are becoming adopted. However, the IT cybersecurity department is also changing. Not only is technology changing, but also our way of working (World Economic Forum 2020, 3).

Technology Threats

Most observers predict new threats coming from new technologies (e.g., 5G, the cloud, APIs, IoT/AI-IoT, *aaS providers, blockchain, AI, digital assistants, and smartphones). This book is not about the specific technologies we are interested in; instead, emerging technologies are often sources of vulnerabilities, with many coming from bad actors and human error (e.g., cloud misconfigurations). The barrage of attacks on new technologies results in a narrow window to patch. Nation-state threats will continue and become more innovative as criminal gangs partner and collaborate to become more effective. Additionally, we are less concerned about the nature of the threat (e.g., malware, phishing, denial of service, and password attacks) and more troubled that new technologies bring new vulnerabilities and new methods of cybercrime.

Targets of Threats

Organizations are increasingly being targeted by adopting more technologies with potentially more vulnerabilities. The human attack surface is also increasing due to the pervasiveness of IoT/AI-IoT devices, ever-broadening global hyperconnectivity, and a pivot to remote work. Cyberattacks are more sophisticated with attempts to control computer systems to immobilize, disturb, or control the technology. For example, we may see more weak-link data exfiltration attacks along organizations' supply chains. Unfortunately, the speed and scale of cyberattacks are growing exponentially, resulting in alert fatigue among frontline cyber-defenders (Microsoft 2020, 25).

Cybersecurity Strategy Is Evolving

Chief information security officers (CISOs) are responsible for developing and managing their cybersecurity strategy. Developing a cybersecurity strategy can be daunting when "cyber-adversaries maintain an advantage over defenders" (Oltsik 2020, 7). Adding to the challenge is that new technologies are in a constant state of development and adoption. This accelerated change results in best practices being slow to emerge to offer guidance (Howard 2020, 3). The result is CISOs need to be creative when developing their strategy.

While CISOs are addressing immediate cyber threats, some are beginning to think about bad actors acquiring and using quantum computing power to facilitate their attacks resulting in an asymmetric advantage (Creese et al. 2020, 44). Others agree it is likely that the advances in technology "will overwhelm many current defenses" (Creese et al. 2020, 44). We see a trend that human involvement in cyberattacks (perpetrators and defenders) is decreasing; that is, machine learning algorithms and deep neural nets are being created to attack vulnerabilities, and defenders rely on these technologies to thwart the attacks since humans "cannot interact fast enough" (Creese et al. 2020, 30). Therefore, we see some CISOs moving away from 100 percent protection to supporting innovation with new technologies that have inherent risks to be competitive (Scholtz 2021, 11); that is, they are reducing their effort to remove 100 percent vulnerabilities and to improve their threat detection and response capabilities (Scholtz, 2021). We may see more emphasis on endpoint security solutions automated with AI and machine learning to detect and block malicious endpoint behavior (CyberEdge Group, LLC 2020, 26) and the emergence of cybersecurity mesh architectures (Groombridge 2021, 3).

Delivery Expectations Are More Stringent

Cybersecurity budgets are increasing to support cybersecurity strategy with expectations for improved governance through metrics related to cybersecurity activity and business success indicators to ensure that our cybersecurity investments are efficient and of high value (Scholtz 2021, 9). Indeed, there is a trend toward risk quantification to prioritize and target cybersecurity investments. Our CISOs commit to the board to deliver projects on time and on budget and manage change effectively and efficiently to bring innovation through the project pipeline (Hale 2017, 364; Scholtz 2021, 9). Effective and efficient project management is the key to CISOs delivering what was promised.

Business Partner Opportunities Emerge

To achieve project success, we are encouraged to become more businesslike by supporting business outcomes rather than only protecting digital assets (Scholtz 2021, 4). We need to buy into business goals as if they were our own. That is, we need to move beyond technology; cybersecurity is increasingly seen holistically not only as a technical problem but also as a business problem as organizations become more mature with cybersecurity management (Hale 2017, 361–362). To be truly effective in our cybersecurity roles, we are encouraged to move beyond our technical focus and think like a CISO to improve our decision making (Scholtz 2021, 9); that is, we need to "learn the business inside and out" (Dhasarathy et al. 2020, 3). Therefore, *Shields Up* includes business-oriented exercises, microlearning, and career planning to assist the reader in developing a balanced set of competencies.

Cybersecurity Budget Increases

Generally, we will see IT budgets continue to grow as organizations put more resources into projects that deliver disruption, innovation, and transformation (Moyer 2021, 3). It is not enough to implement technology; those technologies need to be managed and secured. Therefore, we see predictions that cybersecurity budgets will continue to increase (Claus 2017, 10; CyberEdge Group, LLC 2020, 20). Indeed, cybersecurity spending seems to be a never-ending cyber-arms race (CyberEdge Group, LLC 2020, 9). One concludes that cybersecurity awareness and importance to the organization have also increased given cybersecurity budgets.

One challenge with increased budgets is that demand for cybersecurity services exceeds capacity, putting innovation projects in jeopardy (Oltsik 2020, 42). While cybersecurity budgets are increasing, CISOs are asked to do more with less (Scholtz 2021, 14); it appears that the demand for cybersecurity services can exceed the approved budgets for some organizations. CISOs are required to show value for the money spent on cybersecurity through KPIs and balanced scorecards, focusing on efficient and effective delivery of cybersecurity services and projects. Therefore, increased cybersecurity spending adds additional cybersecurity resources (if you can find them) and new initiatives often delivered through projects: more cybersecurity spending, more cybersecurity projects, and more emphasis on delivering and measuring value.

Cybersecurity Regulation Expands

We can expect more cybersecurity regulation (Creese et al. 2020, 37) for many reasons, such as the increase in the number of cyberattacks and the severity of damage cyberattacks can inflict. For example, AustCyber (2020, 1) estimates that a four-week disruption to the Australian economy due to a cyberattack could cost AUS $30 billion and a 163,000 job loss. The finance industry has recognized the magnitude of this potential loss: "Malicious actors are taking advantage of this digital transformation and pose a growing threat to the global financial system, financial stability, and confidence in the integrity of the financial system. Malign actors are using cyber capabilities to steal from, disrupt, or otherwise threaten financial institutions, investors, and the public" (Maurer and Nelson 2020, 8). Maurer and Nelson (2020, 13 and 35) recommend more government regulation and cooperation to strengthen and protect the global financial system.

Others predict cybersecurity regulations will become more stringent with heavier fines and shorter implementation times (Peacock 2020, 1). The Cybersecurity Act reinforces the European Union's regulations and establishes a certification program for goods and services (European Commission 2021a, 1). Indeed, the United States has released an executive order to improve cybersecurity for all Federal agencies by "making bold changes and significant investments" (White House 2021, 1). Again, we predict more technology, cybersecurity attacks, and regulation. Unfortunately, cybersecurity regulation can be complex, fragmented, and conflicting, making compliance difficult (Pipikaite, Barrachin, and Crawford 2021, 2).

Not only are cybersecurity regulations increasing, but their reach is also broadening. As machine learning cybersecurity activity increases, governments and agencies are becoming more aware of adversarial machine learning and are developing certification frameworks in response. For example, ISO and National Institute of Standards and Technology (NIST) are forming "certification rubrics" to assess the trustworthiness of machine learning (Microsoft 2020, 35). Such actions can lead to additional regulations related to machine learning.

There are longstanding regulations related to cybersecurity, such as the Health Insurance Portability and Accountability Act (HIPAA) and the Gramm–Leach–Bliley Act (GLBA) (Warsinske, Mark, and Kevin 2020, 156). More American cybersecurity regulations are on their way (Tucker 2020, 1), especially after the massive ransomware attacks on Colonial Pipeline and JBS (Marks 2021, 1). The Australian government is in the process of gathering feedback about the direction of cybersecurity regulations that are aligned with international programs, voluntary, and incentive based (Australian Government 2021, 1). The European Commission advocates for strengthened legislation and certification across the EU due to the interconnected nature of the European Union (European Commission 2021b, 2). Therefore, due to the scale and frequency of cyberattacks, many commentators call for more government legislation and regulations (Creese et al. 2020, 37), with cyber-insurance requirements becoming more prescriptive.

Microlearning

Following are exercises to enhance your learning and professional development:

- Identify your organization's cybersecurity regulations.
- What can you expect from your industry and cybersecurity regulation investigation in the next two to five years? Understanding what may be coming to your industry may help you proactively prepare for new cybersecurity regulations.
- Search for "how to conduct a cybersecurity audit." Consider asking your manager to lead an audit project.
- Look for cybersecurity audit tools and checklists.

Cybersecurity Maturity Advancement

Cybersecurity maturity models allow an organization to assess its current capabilities and position them at different levels. By developing a cybersecurity capability baseline, organizations can identify gaps and targets to reach. Currently, many cybersecurity maturity models (Table 3.1) have been compared and analyzed (Payette, Anegbe, Caceres, and Muegge 2015, 1–9; Rea-Guamán, San Feliu, Calvo-Manzano, and Sanchez-Garcia 2017, 1–15; Garba, Siraj, and Othman 2020, 1–8).

Numerous cybersecurity maturity models exist, such as the NIST (see Chapter 4) and the Cybersecurity Capability Maturity Model (C2M2). The C2M2 can be used by any organization of any size or type to evaluate its cybersecurity position and make improvements (U.S. Department of Energy 2021, 12). The C2M2 model has 5 objectives, 10 domains, and 3 maturity levels that an organization can use to assess its cybersecurity maturity (Figure 3.1).

One can conduct an audit to assess the organization's maturity level for each of the 10 domains. Analyzing the audit results, leadership can prioritize and establish maturity improvement targets for prioritized domains. Achieving these improvement goals can trigger new cybersecurity projects.

Objectives

1. Manage IT and OT Asset Inventory
2. Manage Information Asset Inventory
3. Manage Asset Configuration

4. Manage Changes to Assets
5. Management Activities

Domains

1. Risk Management
2. Asset Change and Configuration Management
3. Identity and Access Management
4. Threat and Vulnerability Management
5. Situational Awareness
6. Information Sharing and Communications
7. Event and Incident Response, Continuity of Operations
8. Supply Chain and External Dependencies Management
9. Workforce Management
10. Cybersecurity Program Management

Maturity Levels

1. Initiated
2. Performed
3. Managed

Figure 3.1 C2M2 structure

Organizational Cybersecurity Certification

Some organizations may be required to become certified within a cybersecurity maturity model given the increasing and persistent cybersecurity threats and accompanying regulation efforts. For example, over 300,000 contractors and subcontractors work with the U.S. Department of Defense; most contractors require level 3 CMMC certification for contract eligibility (Horan 2020, 1; Fox 2021, 2). Those contractors who work with the U.S. Department of Energy will also need to certify against the C2M2 soon (Schwartz 2019, 1). To sell to the U.S. federal government, some technology manufacturers must be NIST compliant (Allied Telesis 2021, 1). Therefore, expect organizations to comply with frameworks and subsequent auditing increasingly; both sources of cybersecurity projects are coming our way!

Cybersecurity Skill Shortage

The very nature of work is changing due to a "reskilling revolution" where the shelf life of people's skills is reduced, requiring regular upskilling (Skulmoski, Langston, Patching, and Ghanbaripour 2020, 3). Organizations report challenges finding competent people (World Economic

Table 3.1 Cybersecurity maturity models

Model	Focus
National Institute of Standards and Technology Cybersecurity Framework (NIST CSF)	The NIST CSF was first released in 2014 and includes five functions and five "implementation tiers" (e.g., maturity levels)
C2M2	First published in 1996 by the U.S. National Security Agency, it includes 129 base practices across 22 process areas, with five maturity levels
Electricity Subsector Cybersecurity Capability Maturity Model (ES-C2M2)	The U.S. Department of Energy introduced the ES-C2M2, a subset of the C2M2 model focused on energy
Oil and Natural Gas Subsector Cybersecurity Capability Maturity Model (ONG-C2M2)	The ONG-C2M2 was designed specifically for the oil and gas sector with five maturity levels and is a subset of the C2M2
Community Cyber Security Maturity Model (CCSMM)	Developed by the Center for Infrastructure Assurance and security in 2006, it includes five maturity levels
National Initiative for Cybersecurity Education (NICE)-Capability Maturity Model	The NICE-Capability Maturity Model was established in 2008 to develop cybersecurity staff and has three maturity levels
ES-C2M2	The U.S. Department of Energy released their ES-C2M2 in 2012 with 10 domains and 3 maturity levels
Federal Financial Institute of Examination Council-Capability Maturity Model (FFIEC-CMM)	The FFIEC-CMM was released in 2014 to guide financial institutions to improve their cybersecurity. The model has five domains and five maturity levels
African Union Maturity Model for Cybersecurity (AUMMCS)	The AUMMCS was introduced in 2014 and had three domains and four maturity levels
Systems Security Engineering Capability Maturity Model (SSE-CMM)	A descriptive model published in 2014 by the U.S. Department of Energy and is organized into 10 domains with 4 maturity levels
Computer Security Incident Response Team (CSIRT)	The European Union Agency for Network and Information Security (ENISA) published the CSIRT maturity model with three tiers and four categories
Cybersecurity Maturity Model Certification (CMMC)	The U.S. Department of Defense has implemented the CMMC framework to normalize and standardize the federal government's defense industrial base. The model has 5 levels, 43 capabilities, and 171 practices
CERT Resilience Management Model (CERT-RMM)	The CERT RMM guides organizations to assess business continuity, security, and IT operations

Forum 2020, 11). The digital disruption leads to digital skills gaps generally and for project managers to implement digital projects (PMI 2018, 6). Experts predict a sustained shortage of global project management talent through the next decade (PMI 2017b) exacerbated by the increase in demand for competent cybersecurity project positions (Oltsik 2020, 49). There is a shortage of project managers, but what about the cybersecurity skills shortage?

Finding qualified cybersecurity professionals is one of the most challenging of all technical professions (Morgan 2019, 4–6). "Simply put, it is more difficult to hire security professionals today than it was even three or four years ago" (Scholtz 2021, 13); indeed, the cybersecurity profession has been characterized as in a deepening "crisis" (Oltsik 2020, 5). The unemployment rate for cybersecurity professionals is zero percent and has been so since 2011 (Morgan 2019, 6). The high demand for cybersecurity professionals has attracted unqualified applicants where less than one in four were qualified (Morgan 2019, 2).

Compounding the problem of the cybersecurity skills gap is that the cybersecurity role is changing to align with changing technologies and stakeholder expectations (Scholtz 2021, 14). We see specializations such as security strategist, vulnerability analyst, machine learning cyber analyst, cyber lawyer, and cybersecurity project manager. Now CISOs face a dual problem related to cybersecurity staffing: not only is it challenging to find suitable talent, but the cybersecurity job requirements are also shifting to account for future needs (Scholtz 2021, 14).

One strategy to mitigate the cybersecurity skills shortage is to delegate some cybersecurity functions to the business, corporate, and other IT teams (Scholtz 2021, 15). An emerging corporate value is everyone has a role in cybersecurity since the technology ecosystem is hyperconnected and complex (Morgan 2019, 2). For example, we may see our HR training unit provide cybersecurity awareness training to all staff rather than having a cybersecurity SME deliver the training. We cascade cybersecurity tasks to others where low-complexity cybersecurity projects are assigned to competent technical team members rather than an experienced project manager.

There is a shortage of cybersecurity project managers resulting in a strong demand today that will continue in the future (Oltsik 2020, 36).

Rather than waiting for a project manager to become available to lead a routine cybersecurity project, cybersecurity project managers are assigned to more challenging and critical projects, leaving routine cybersecurity projects assigned to nonproject manager roles. Indeed, some recommend that IT departments provide training to technical staff ranging from "business, communications, leadership, and management skills" (e.g., managing projects and initiatives) (Oltsik 2020, 45).

Profession in Crisis

Our cybersecurity profession is in crisis. Not only is there more technology to protect, but the technology is also becoming increasingly complex, resulting in an increased demand for cybersecurity services (Figure 3.2). The skills gap is especially exasperated in new cybersecurity technologies (Howard 2020, 5).

Additionally, there are other skill gap drivers, such as poor strategic planning by the organization and inadequate career planning by the individual. Finally, the cybersecurity role is changing from a technical focus to a broader role as a business partner that requires a broader skillset. Thus, there are many drivers of the cybersecurity skills gap.

The impact of the cybersecurity skills gap is multifold and far reaching. Due to unfilled cybersecurity positions and increased demand for cybersecurity services, the workload assigned to cybersecurity professionals is heavy and can be stressful (Oltsik 2020, 21). A direct result of the increased workload is that cybersecurity professionals find it challenging to keep up with their learning about new technologies and to learn to use existing cybersecurity tools to their full potential resulting in increased risks for the organization (Oltsik 2020, 37). The cybersecurity skills gaps continue to impede organizational cybersecurity.

Organizational Role

There are many ways organizations can mitigate the cybersecurity skills gap challenge. Since cybersecurity professionals are under constant pressure to remain competent and knowledgeable about cybersecurity, they struggle to find the time to develop new skills (Claus 2017, 8).

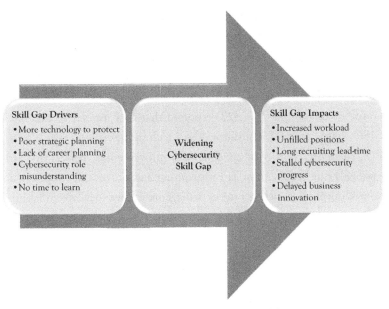

Figure 3.2 Cybersecurity skills gap shortage model

Therefore, organizations can anticipate the skills shortage and support existing personnel in planning their cybersecurity careers and providing training and development opportunities (Howard 2020, 6; Oltsik 2020, 20). Forward-thinking cybersecurity professionals will actively leverage this knowledge to plan their careers with managers and mentors.

Opportunity: Organizations are advised to provide more support to technical staff such as training and development opportunities; therefore, discuss career development with your manager or human resources. They might provide premium-quality training and education funding and help with career pathways such as secondments and lateral moves. Your organization wants you to succeed!

Cybersecurity Career Planning

It should not come as a surprise that busy cybersecurity professionals often neglect career planning when they routinely work long and stressful hours. Instead, cybersecurity professionals often take an informal and haphazard career management approach; however, cybersecurity professionals are encouraged to take a systematic approach to career planning with a transformation coach and develop holistically (Oltsik 2020, 45). Too often, cybersecurity professionals have a tactical focus (Oltsik 2020, 45) and chase certifications to develop technically. Focusing solely on developing technical expertise seems counterintuitive when 47 percent of security professionals (sample $N = 327$) reported that they aspired to become a CISO that is more of a business than a technical position (Oltsik 2020, 17). Therefore, as part of continuous improvement, cybersecurity professionals can benefit from career planning and broader development in nontechnical areas such as project management. (See the Career Planning in Appendix 4.)

Future of Cybersecurity: Final Thoughts

Cybersecurity threats are increasing and becoming more innovative, with more targets. Organizations are responding with updated strategies and increased budgets to harden their security. Organizations face increased cybersecurity regulations, especially if they intend to operate within government procurement programs. As cybersecurity threats evolve, cybersecurity strategy is evolving, and organizations increasingly plan their cybersecurity maturity journey. However, while many have healthy budgets, leadership expects IT departments to deliver their projects on time and on budget. Thus, we have a cybersecurity skills shortage (technical and project management) that challenges organizations.

CHAPTER 4

Technical Framework Alignment

Few organizations provide IT and cybersecurity services in isolation; that is, they often follow best practices and frameworks to provide quality services and products. Organizations follow external frameworks for cybersecurity operations and projects to guide quality, technology, cybersecurity, and project delivery (see Figure 4.1).

All frameworks are aligned with a focus on satisfying the customer by predictably delivering products and services to the right level of quality, with continuous quality improvement driving innovation; delivering and optimizing value are common aims in these frameworks and standards.

Quality Management: Cornerstone of Compliance

What is quality management? According to International Organization for Standardization (ISO) 9004, quality policies and processes are established to achieve objectives through quality planning, quality assurance, control, and continuous improvement to make up the quality management system (ISO 2000, 10). Continuous improvement is fundamental to providing services valued by the end-user and is maximized if a continual improvement mindset is adopted by all project stakeholders (Limited, AXELOS 2019, 71). Project quality management includes those processes to plan, manage, and control the project and the project's product or service to meet our stakeholder's objectives (e.g., to provide something of value). Project quality management also includes continuous process improvement (PMI 2017a, 271). Information Technology Infrastructure Library (ITIL), ISO, and Project Management Institute (PMI) quality management guidance are closely related; the PMI focuses on quality management within the project context, while ISO quality management

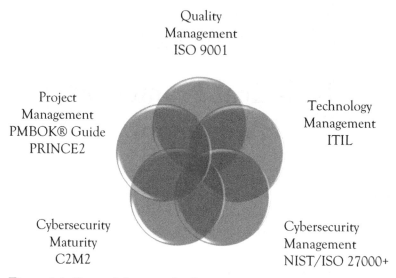

Quality
Management
ISO 9001

Project
Management
PMBOK® Guide
PRINCE2

Technology
Management
ITIL

Cybersecurity
Maturity
C2M2

Cybersecurity
Management
NIST/ISO 27000+

Figure 4.1 External framework alignment

is more general. Therefore, these standards are aligned, and complying with one brings you close to complying with the other standards regarding quality management.

Quality management underpins best practices and standards related to project management, service management, and cybersecurity services. After planning how quality will be managed in the project, quality management can be seen as a three-step process: (a) quality assurance, (b) do the work, and (c) quality control (Figure 4.2).

Quality assurance aims to provide confidence the quality requirements will be met. Most standards (e.g., ISO, NIST, and C2M2) guide organizations to include quality assurance and control activities. Organizations provide training, templates, checklists, and processes to deliver the right quality. Then, we perform the work such as configuring a virtual server by following a checklist. After the work is performed, we conduct quality control: finding and fixing defects. Again, we rely upon training, templates, and checklists and follow processes to determine whether the right quality was delivered. We have an A-B-C approach to quality management: quality Assurance, Before, quality Control. The quality management process is seen in leading standards across industries; therefore, applying this simple quality management approach, you will

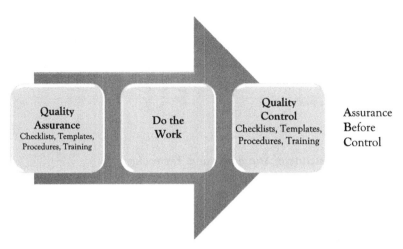

Figure 4.2 Quality management process

likely be compliant with most quality domains, in most standards, most of the time. Expect regulators and insurance companies to request regular audits for cybersecurity specifically and technology generally. Auditing can be a type of quality control project (e.g., NIST Framework auditing and compliance process). Leading an audit project would be suitable for developing new project management capabilities and increasing one's holistic understanding of the technology ecosystem.

Cybersecurity Frameworks

A cybersecurity framework is a collection of standards, guidelines, and best practices to manage cybersecurity risks. Frameworks can improve reliability and predictability. Two leading cybersecurity standards are briefly presented with linkages to the vital role project management has in meeting these standards:

1. NIST Framework for Improving Critical Infrastructure Cybersecurity;
2. ISO 27000 Series for Information Security Controls.

These standards are widely adopted, and their influence is growing. They include an entire strategy life cycle from projects to operations with a continuous improvement orientation bringing new projects, new opportunities, and new services. Organizations use frameworks to identify areas to strengthen or new processes to implement. Organizations that follow these frameworks may be better positioned to manage the increasing demand for cybersecurity projects following continuous improvement practices.

National Institute of Standards and Technology Cybersecurity Framework

The highly regarded NIST Framework for Improving Critical Infrastructure Cybersecurity is intended to protect critical infrastructures like transport, health, energy, food, water, communications, banking, and finance (National Institute of Standards and Technology 2018, 5). The NIST Framework guides cybersecurity for critical infrastructures. It can be used by any organization striving for better cybersecurity: "While this document was developed to improve cybersecurity risk management in critical infrastructure, the Framework can be used by organizations in any sector or community. The Framework enables organizations—regardless of size, degree of cybersecurity risk, or cybersecurity sophistication—to apply the principles and best practices of risk management to improving security and resilience" (National Institute of Standards and Technology 2018, 5).

The basics of cybersecurity defense are to protect the organization's assets through five functions and related categories (Figure 4.3). You may be asked to participate and lead projects in any of these areas; the sources of cybersecurity projects are vast.

Figure 4.3 NIST Cybersecurity Framework: functions and categories

The categories reveal the scope of cybersecurity objectives and are supported by 108 subcategories (see Appendix 1 for an example of the framework core). Within this framework of functions, categories, and subcategories, we better understand where we are today and where our organizational improvement targets lie. The NIST Framework includes implementation tiers designed to provide a path toward cybersecurity maturity and target achievement (Figure 4.4, after National Institute of Standards and Technology 2018, 15–17).

Figure 4.4 NIST cybersecurity capability maturity levels

Organizations use the NIST Framework to document their current profile of cybersecurity (Figure 4.5, after PMI 2021, 6) and then initiate projects to take them to the target profile (e.g., address gaps in Tier 3, or progress from Tier 3 to Tier 4, or to comply with an external agency's NIST-based guidelines). Thus, we can expect projects to improve the organization's capabilities within these categories and from organizations implementing projects to mature through the NIST maturity tiers. *Shields Up* will help you plan, manage, and deliver projects to progress through the NIST maturity tiers.

Figure 4.5 Cybersecurity improvement through projects

The NIST Framework is aligned with project management, and following a formal project management method helps you comply with the Framework. The NIST Framework includes a project-oriented section—Establishing or Improving a Cybersecurity Program—bringing the organization to its target profile through a project delivery approach (National Institute of Standards and Technology 2018, 21–22). This book helps you plan and implement NIST Framework-related cybersecurity projects.

ISO 27001: Information Security Management

The ISO 27000 (ISO 2013b) is a set of information security standards to plan, implement, maintain, and improve the organization's information security management system (see Figure 4.6 for an overview of the ISO 27000 standard). Often, organizations begin with an informal and disorganized approach to cybersecurity and then adopt a standard like ISO 27000 to manage information security threats systematically (ISO 2013a, 1–32).

The ISO 27001 requirements are ordered into 114 controls where each addresses a specific cybersecurity risk (e.g., securing application services on public networks). These controls are categorized into 14 annexes/groups (beginning with Annex 5) seen in Figure 4.6. These controls guide organizations to improve their cybersecurity. Organizations can determine current and target profiles as part of their continuous improvement efforts.

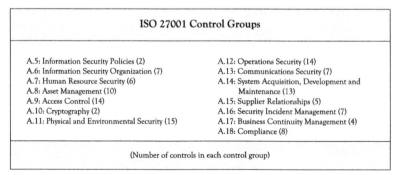

Figure 4.6 ISO information security standards

Of particular interest is control A.14 System Acquisition, Development, and Maintenance since it includes project management activities such as:

A.14.2 Security in Development and Support Processes: design in cybersecurity;

A.14.2.7 Outsourced Development: manage outsourced projects to ensure the right quality of cybersecurity;

A.14.2.8 System Security Testing: test security functionality;

A.14.2.9 System Acceptance Testing: test that the systems are built as designed, including information security testing and compliance with best practices.

This book aligns with the project management-related controls in this standard. Therefore, following this project management approach will help you comply with ISO 27001 information security management.

Indeed, project management is the implied delivery vehicle for many cybersecurity projects: "Information security shall be addressed in project management, regardless of the type of the project" (ISO 2018a, 10). Information security in the ISO cybersecurity standard is intertwined with project management language such as "to ensure information security is *designed and implemented* within the development life cycle of information systems" (ISO 2018a, 18). Information systems go through a systems life cycle: they are initiated, specified, designed, developed, tested, implemented, used, maintained, and eventually retired from service and disposed of (ISO 2018a, vii). The "initiate" through to "implemented" mirrors the project life cycle, whereas "used" through to "disposed of" reflects operations. We see both the project and operations life cycles in the ISO standard. Since project management is inherent in the ISO 27000 Information Security Management suite of standards, one will be more successful in implementing cybersecurity projects when one becomes proficient with project management.

The ISO 27000 family of cybersecurity standards is comprehensive but lacks a maturity model; instead, the ISO cybersecurity standard can be considered the top level of a maturity model—level five (Leal 2015, 2). One finds traditional, waterfall project management firmly embedded in the ISO 27000 information security standard with only a cursory review of the standard. Delivering cybersecurity projects using the traditional project management delivery approach and tools will align your project with the ISO 27000 family of cybersecurity standards and improve the probability of project success.

Information Technology Infrastructure Library (Limited, AXELOS)

IT departments provide IT services like e-mails, human resource applications, productivity applications, and security for the IT ecosystem for their organizations. IT leadership establishes policies and procedures to guide life-cycle management of the technology ecosystem. Often, IT leadership relies on external standards and frameworks to guide their actions. The promise is that if an organization follows a framework, business activities can become more predictable and stable while maintaining the desired level of quality. One of the significant IT frameworks followed by organizations is the ITIL. While other IT frameworks exist (e.g., COBIT and ISO IEC 20000), ITIL might be the most popular and widely adopted.

ITIL Overview

What is ITIL? It is a framework of best practices to deliver and manage IT services like threat detection, e-mail, and project management. ITIL provides a comprehensive, holistic, and systematic approach to delivering value, managing risks and quality, implementing lean practices, and building a predictable and stable technical ecosystem supporting growth and resilience. ITIL can guide teams to automate processes, improve IT services, and integrate technology into business practices. The ITIL way of delivering and managing technology is one of the most popular globally (Berger, Shashidhar, and Varol 2020, 1) and therefore is considered the global de facto standard (Tsunoda and Kino 2018, 1). The ITIL way of technology management is the theoretical foundation in *Shields Up* upon which we build a hybrid project management approach to cybersecurity projects.

ITIL prominence has attracted research interest (Berger et al. 2020, 1–6; Göbel and Cronholm 2015, 1–22; Marrone and Kolbe 2011, 363–380; Ramakrishnan 2014, 159–168), and the following benefits of ITIL have been identified:

- Improved IT services by following proven best practices and processes (Göbel and Cronholm 2015, 6).
- Improved benefits realization as ITIL adoption matures (Marrone and Kolbe 2011, 377).
- Improved customer satisfaction by delivering services that meet business needs (Marrone, Kiessling, and Kolbe 2010, 381).
- Improved productivity such as first call resolution gains (Marrone et al. 2010, 378; Berger et al. 2020, 1).
- Improved communications through common terminology (Göbel and Cronholm 2015, 6).
- Improved return on investment (Marrone et al. 2010, 378).
- Reduced IT costs (Göbel and Cronholm 2015, 6).

ITIL is widely adopted and growing in part due to the potential benefits; indeed, we see statements like "ITIL Foundation is the most widely held certification this year" (Global Knowledge 2021, 22). Even if your organization has not formally implemented ITIL, you may be following ITIL practices such as incident management because ITIL practices are considered best practices (Zaydi and Nassereddine 2020, 1; Sliep and Marnewick 2020, 4).

ITIL v4, released in 2019, is a major departure from the previous versions. It reshapes the relationship with customers, processes, and value and embraces new ways of working like lean management and agile project management. ITIL 4 takes a strategic and holistic approach to meeting organizational needs through the Service Value Chain to deliver value to the user of the ITIL service (Limited, AXELOS 2019, 66). ITIL 4 focuses on the entire life cycle of the service called the Service Value Chain.

ITIL Service Value Chain

Organizations begin their ITIL journey by considering the ITIL Service Value Chain (Figure 4.7). The value stream is a process to create and deliver products and services to consumers (Limited, AXELOS 2019, 66). Simply, the Service Value Chain process begins when an opportunity or need triggers a new service (e.g., a project).

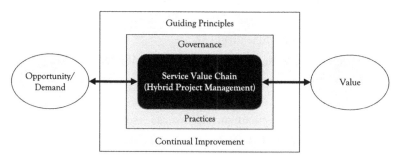

Figure 4.7 ITIL service value chain

The six Service Value Chain activities include the following (Limited, AXELOS 2019, 66):

1. **Plan**: Arrive at a shared understanding of the project scope and the four dimensions of service (discussed later).
2. **Improve**: Continuously improve the products, services, and processes across the value chain and four dimensions.
3. **Engage**: Develop good relationships with stakeholders to understand their requirements better.
4. **Design and transition**: Implement products and services that meet the stakeholders' expectations for quality, costs, and time to market.
5. **Obtain/build**: Provide the service or product when and where each is required.
6. **Deliver and support**: Support the products and services to the agreed requirements and performance specifications.

While these Service Value Chain activities appear to be sequential, the planning, continuous improvement, and engaging stakeholders activities occur throughout the Service Value Chain process.

These Service Value Chain activities occur within the context of four dimensions of service management that offer insight into different perspectives of service management. These dimensions of service management need to be planned and managed at a micro (project) level through to a macro (organization) level of service (Limited, AXELOS 2019, 36):

1. **Organizations and people**: The Service Value Chain activities occur in an organizational setting and through the effort of people. The organization's governance and communications systems must be considered when planning and executing activities (e.g., a cybersecurity project).

2. **Information and technology**: The required information, knowledge, and technology are considered when planning and delivering Service Value Chain activities. One considers the feasibility and impact of the information, knowledge, and technology dimension to manage and deliver the service. The information and technology dimension is central to most cybersecurity projects.

3. **Partners and suppliers**: The relationship with other organizations is considered when planning and executing Service Value Chain activities. Outsourcing, partnering, and other relationships with external SMEs are common in cybersecurity projects and are considered in cybersecurity projects.

4. **Value streams and processes**: The organization's value streams and processes are those activities and processes we follow to deliver services and products valued by the user. In this dimension, we are guided to become lean and responsive to change.

Managing work within these ITIL 4 dimensions from a holistic perspective will improve project success since we do not work in isolation; these dimensions impact our cybersecurity projects. When planning our cybersecurity projects, we may consider these four dimensions—risks, issues, assumptions, and constraints.

Like other standards and frameworks, ITIL 4 includes principles to guide our decisions and actions when completing work in the Service Value Chain. When organizations adopt these principles, they increase the likelihood of a common approach to delivering services and products.

These principles apply to most Service Value Chain activities (Limited, AXELOS 2019, 47–48):

1. **Focus on value**: Ensure all activities create value, directly or indirectly, to the organization, users, and/or other stakeholders.
2. **Start where you are**: Apply lean thinking to value chain activities, optimizing existing products and services before throwing away what exists and introducing a new project. We look to leverage what is available to reduce waste through a systematic process to measure, observe, and improve (the Lean Six Sigma method aligns neatly with this principle).
3. **Progress iteratively with feedback**: Deliver services incrementally, if possible, rather than all at once to reduce risk and improve the probability of successfully delivering the intended value. Therefore, look for opportunities to break up your cybersecurity projects into multiple, smaller projects (e.g., phases 1 and 2). Build-in regular feedback opportunities to ensure value is being delivered.
4. **Collaborate and promote visibility**: We deliver services through the Service Value Chain, often in teams where collaboration can lead to improved engagement, support, commitment, lasting outcomes, understanding, trust, and cooperation. Sharing visibility also contributes to these positive outcomes.
5. **Think and work holistically**: Value is improved when delivered conceptually as a full service or product, rather than individual components. Value is increased when the Service Value System (SVS, Figure 4.7), four dimensions of service management, and these principles are coordinated and integrated. Visibility into the entire service value stream improves understanding, management, and control. The think-and-work holistically principle is good cybersecurity practice.
6. **Keep it simple and practical**: We endeavor to complete Service Value Chain activities with a minimum number of steps. Lean thinking is encouraged.
7. **Optimize and automate**: We look for opportunities to improve the Service Value Chain to maximize the value of services and products we deliver. Increasingly, we use technology and automation and quality improvement methods like the Lean Six Sigma DMAIC process to guide improvements.

These principles are foundational in that they should guide the organization in all circumstances, even if there are changes to organizational goals, personnel, project type, and so on. The ITIL principles are intended to shape organizational culture in all activities (e.g., projects and operations) along the Service Value Chain (Limited, AXELOS 2019, 17–18).

ITIL 4 includes practices representing capabilities used to create value in the Service Value Chain (Table 4.1). ITIL 4 has published practice guides to provide resources for service management; think of the practices as a toolkit you use in the service management system to deliver value. The ITIL practices can be mapped to the traditional project management delivery method used in technology projects to illustrate their approximate relationship including the Transition to Production (T2P) phase.

Thus, ITIL 4 has a comprehensive and holistic framework to manage technology services such as cybersecurity projects. ITIL 4 supports tailoring the framework to the organization, context, and project; hybrid project management is supported: "the ITIL SVS supports many approaches such as agile, DevOps and Lean, as well as traditional process and project management, with a flexible value-oriented operating model" (Limited, AXELOS 2019, 44). ITIL 4 provides a comprehensive service management framework that aligns with hybrid project management.

Information Systems Development Life Cycle

If ITIL looks familiar to you, it may be due to ITIL being aligned with sound systems management practices. You are probably familiar with the information systems development life cycle (SDLC) that we learn about in university and college information systems subjects. The life cycle is process-based and iterative, designed to deliver quality systems to support business and customer expectations, much like ITIL. Thus, the SDLC takes a process-oriented approach with an iterative quality improvement life cycle (Figure 4.8). The SDLC includes project activities (planning through to implementing) and operational activities (operations, maintenance, and optimization).

This traditional approach to systems development is also known as the waterfall model. It has been modified to provide alternative ways to develop systems such as the spiral model, V-model, rapid application development, rational unified process, and agile delivery methods (Sekgweleo 2015, 52).

Table 4.1 ITIL practices mapped to project phases

Practice	Initiate	Plan	Design	Build	Test	T2P	Monitor	Close Out	Operate	Improve
General management practices										
1. Architecture management			✓							
2. Continual improvement								✓		✓
3. Security management			✓							
4. Knowledge management						✓		✓		
5. Measurement and reporting		✓								
6. Organizational change management						✓				
7. Portfolio management	✓	✓	✓	✓	✓	✓	✓	✓		
8. Project management	✓	✓	✓	✓	✓	✓	✓	✓		
9. Relationship management		✓	✓							
10. Risk management	✓	✓	✓	✓	✓	✓	✓	✓		
11. Service financial management		✓								
12. Strategy management		✓								
13. Supplier management		✓								
14. Workforce and talent management		✓								
Service management practices										
15. Availability management			✓							
16. Business analysis			✓							

17.	Capacity and performance management		✓					
18.	Change enablement		✓		✓			
19.	Incident management		✓					
20.	IT asset management		✓		✓			
21.	Monitoring and event management		✓		✓			
22.	Problem management		✓					
23.	Release management				✓			
24.	Service catalog management				✓			
25.	Service configuration management				✓			
26.	Service continuity management				✓			
27.	Service design						✓	
28.	Service desk				✓			
29.	Service level management						✓	
30.	Service request management		✓					
31.	Service validation and testing			✓				

Technical management practices

32.	Deployment management				✓			
33.	Infrastructure and platform management				✓			
34.	Software development and management	✓						

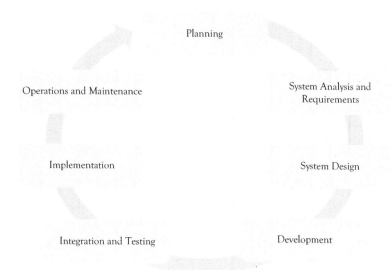

Planning

Operations and Maintenance

System Analysis and
Requirements

Implementation

System Design

Integration and Testing

Development

Figure 4.8 Systems development life cycle

Exercise

Review the ITIL Service Value Chain and compare how closely your organization is aligned to the framework. Which practices do you use and can add to your resume?

When an information systems life-cycle approach is followed, the results are more predictable because the stakeholders understand the steps in the process and can plan accordingly. We are encouraged to build cybersecurity into the SDLC, including threat modeling, design reviews, static and dynamic testing, and penetration testing in the production environment (Microsoft 2020, 75). We see that the SDLC aligns with traditional project management, IT service management, and cybersecurity management best practices and with supporting processes like quality management. *Shields Up* is aligned with the information systems life-cycle approach. Therefore, by following the approaches in this book, you will continue to contribute to good project management, IT, and cybersecurity practices.

Technical Framework Alignment: Final Thoughts

Quality management is fundamental to many frameworks, including cybersecurity. The NIST Cybersecurity Framework is the de facto global framework many organizations use to deliver and optimize cybersecurity services. Cybersecurity services are often delivered within the ITIL framework that follows the Service Value Chain beginning with an identified need or opportunity, delivered to the organization through a project management delivery method that is used and optimized.

CHAPTER 5

Project Management Frameworks

There are two categories of project management frameworks: competency frameworks for individuals and maturity models for organizations. Like cybersecurity capability maturity models, there are project management capability models like PMI's Project Management Maturity Model (ProMMM). Organizations can follow these maturity models to improve their project management capabilities, much like improving capabilities by progressing through cybersecurity tiers. Since cybersecurity professionals are less likely to lead project management improvement projects, ProMMMs are out of scope for this book. Instead, we look at project management frameworks (e.g., The Guide to the Project Management Body of Knowledge [PMBOK® Guide] and PRINCE2) aimed at individuals to guide them in project management.

Multiple project management frameworks can be explained on a continuum of predictive to adaptive project delivery (Figure 5.1). We can use a predictive project management delivery approach to plan our project using schedules, budgets, and other tools to forecast task completion, phase by phase. This traditional approach is sometimes known as waterfall project management since it is sequential and linear; a new phase does not start until the previous phase finishes. Most professional organizations (e.g., the PMI and the International Project Management Association) support predictive approaches to project management.

However, with the increasing popularity of agile project management, project management associations have embraced adaptive project management approaches like the Scrum method in their standards. Agile delivery approaches are appropriate when there is (i) ambiguity about the product or service to be delivered by the project team or (ii) ambiguity about how

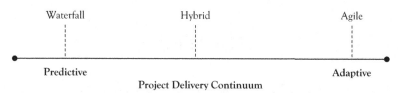

Figure 5.1 Project Delivery Continuum

to deliver the product or service. Complex and ambiguous projects can benefit from an adaptive delivery approach; however, such approaches are out of scope for this book since (i) most cybersecurity projects have low ambiguity (e.g., install new software or conduct an audit), and (ii) the top cybersecurity frameworks (and ISO quality management) imply a traditional or predictive project management approach. Therefore, this book emphasizes the traditional project management delivery approach to help the reader deliver routine cybersecurity projects. However, the hybrid project management approach in *Shields Up* accommodates adaptive project work when sufficient ambiguity or complexity is encountered (e.g., design challenges).

Guide to the Project Management Body of Knowledge

The PMBOK® Guide from the PMI is widely regarded as the de facto global project management standard. The PMBOK® Guide 7th Edition contains the Standard for Project Management and a PMBOK® Guide (Figure 5.2). The 7th Edition is a departure from previous versions: the earlier versions of the PMBOK® Guide directed the reader on *how* to implement a project by following processes like the planning process. The reader would use information in the knowledge areas (e.g., schedule, cost, and quality) during a project management process (e.g., develop a schedule during the planning process). The focus of the PMBOK® Guide (editions 1–6) was tactical (how to plan and deliver projects), while the PMBOK® Guide 7th Edition is strategic (*what* to manage).

Project management principles are emphasized in the 7th Edition of the PMBOK® Guide. Principles are intended to be applied to all projects, regardless of the type and complexity of the project, project manager, and

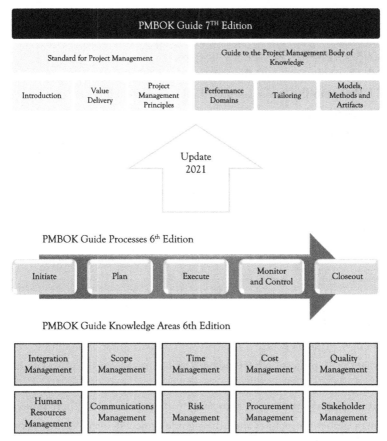

Figure 5.2 PMBOK® Guide Evolution

sponsor. Principles are enduring and universal. The PMBOK® Guide 7th Edition principles guide our behavior in projects (PMI 2021, 42–43):

1. **Stewardship:** Be a diligent, respectful, and caring steward.
2. **Collaborative team:** Build a collaborative project team environment.
3. **Stakeholders:** Effectively engage with stakeholders.
4. **Value:** Focus on value.
5. **Holistic thinking:** Recognize, evaluate, and respond to systems interactions.
6. **Leadership:** Demonstrate leadership behaviors.

7. **Tailoring:** Tailor based on context.

8. **Quality:** Build quality into processes and deliverables.

9. **Complexity:** Navigate complexity.

10. **Opportunities and threats:** Optimize risk responses.

11. **Adaptability and resilience:** Embrace adaptability and resiliency.

12. **Change management:** Enable change to achieve the envisioned future state.

Shields Up is aligned with the processes and knowledge areas of the 6th Edition (e.g., quality and risk management processes from a tactical perspective) and the principles of the 7th Edition (strategic focus) that guide our behavior when we manage projects.

Exercise

These PMBOK® Guide principles are like the Agile Manifesto and ITIL 4 principles; take a moment to compare these principles to see that the IT profession has long been following these principles to guide our work (see agile project management, Figure 5.4). Think about how you complete your work according to these principles. These project management principles and others guide project delivery in the hybrid project management approach in *Shields Up*. Which principles can you prioritize for further development?

Sense of Urgency

Two additional principles guide successful project managers: work with a sense of urgency and front-end load work. If you have ever thought, "I wish I had one more day to ....," then these two other principles will help you deliver on time. Projects become late one day at a time; therefore, we try to maximize at a sustainable pace what we accomplish daily. We see this principle in successful project managers where action-oriented meetings start on time, with shorter durations. Meetings are scheduled for tomorrow rather than next week, and so on. Business and technical leaders notice not only your sense of urgency but also your team. Model a sense of urgency, and this principle will permeate your team's project behavior.

Front-End Loading

The second principle that reduces risks and issues is to front-end load: bringing forward work (where it makes sense) to create space in the future to leverage opportunities or manage risks and issues. Front-end loading is not a new concept but one that is proven to work; my father used to say: "Don't put off until tomorrow what you can do today." We can pull forward low-risk tasks such as setting up your templates (e.g., project charter infographic, design document, PLO duration estimates workbook, schedule, meeting minutes, status reports, T2P tracker, and testing defects register) and booking your meeting rooms (e.g., weekly meeting with the team, risk management meetings, and status meetings). Much of this work can be done after hours when your energy is low (e.g., setting up your team collaboration site). Successful project managers often work overtime at the start of the project; working long hours early in the project is much easier than working long days and weekends at the end of the project when stress is high! Front-end load and you are less likely to wish for one more day. Front-end loading and working with a sense of urgency allows you to learn more about your project sooner in the project life cycle. These two principles are effective and are noticed on projects. Incorporating a sense of urgency, front-end loading, and the PMBOK® Guide's principles into your practice will improve your project success rate and inspire confidence.

PRINCE2

With a search online, one discovers that the PMP certification is widely respected and globally portable; however, the PRINCE2 project management framework is also popular (PRINCE2.com 2021, 1). The UK government first released PRINCE2 (PRojects IN Controlled Environments) to guide public service technology projects in 1989. PRINCE2 includes processes, themes, and principles (Figure 5.3). The PRINCE2 model is prescriptive; the reader is guided about what should be done on the project, when it should be done, and who should complete the task.

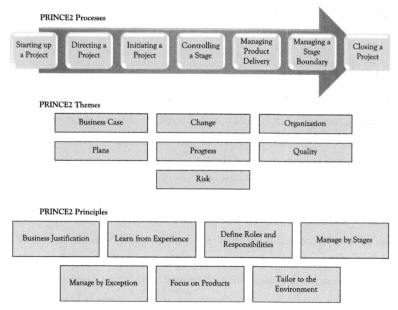

Figure 5.3 PRINCE2 framework

Individuals can get certified in PRINCE2 through the AXELOS organization: PRINCE2 Foundation or the more extensive PRINCE2 Practitioner. When comparing PRINCE2 with the PMBOK® Guide v6 and v7, there are many similarities, such as following processes while guided by principles. The PMBOK® Guides have increasingly included agile components, while the PRINCE2 method expanded to include PRINCE2 Agile. *Shields Up* is aligned with these process-based frameworks and agile principles.

Agile Project Management

Agile project management means different things to different people; some in the business see agile project management as being flexible and nimble in our plans and execution. However, the IT professional may equate agile project management with the Scrum delivery method (Figure 5.4). Agile project management has been widely studied, and its benefits and challenges are increasingly understood (Azanha, Argoud, de Camargo Junior, and Antoniolli 2019, 121–142; Drury, Conboy, and Power 2012,

1239–1254; Gemino, Horner Reich, and Serrador 2021, 161–175; Serrador and Pinto 2015, 1040–1051). Agile project management can be effective under the right circumstances. Agile project management is best used when there is ambiguity in (i) what needs to be delivered or (ii) how to deliver the product or service. We use agile project management when our project faces high volatility and uncertainty (PMI 2021, 101).

A Scrum begins when a product owner (project sponsor) prioritizes work in the product backlog, and the project team selects and plans the amount of work they can complete during one sprint (e.g., typically two weeks to one month). After the team plans the work, the project moves to the sprint cycle, where the product or service is designed, built, tested, and delivered to the product owner. Iterative work and continuous improvement/learning are inherent in agile project management to adapt to changes and feedback to deliver the right amount of value. The team then returns to the prioritized backlog to begin a new sprint with planning.

One can overlay the waterfall project management approach onto the Scrum method (Figure 5.4) to see that the project work is similar in an agile and waterfall approach (e.g., plan, design, and build). Sound project management activities work in either approach: adaptive or predictive project management. Therefore, project management fundamentals are transferable to other project management and managerial approaches.

Agile project work is guided by the Agile Manifesto (Figure 5.5): 4 values and 12 principles (AgileManifesto.org 2001, 1). The Scrum

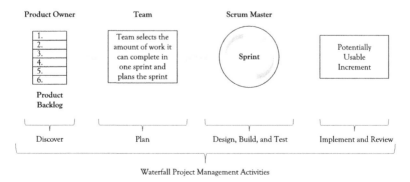

Figure 5.4 Agile project management with the Scrum

Agile Principles

1. Customer satisfaction
2. Accommodate changing requirements
3. Frequent delivery of *value**
4. Collaboration
5. Support, trust, and motivate the people involved
6. Enable face-to-face interactions
7. Working *deliverables*** is the primary measure of progress
8. Consistent work pace
9. Attention to technical detail and design
10. Simplicity
11. Self-organizing teams
12. Lessons learned

Agile Manifesto

Agile Manifesto Values

Individuals and Interactions over Tools and Processes	Working Software over Comprehensive Documentation	Customer Collaboration over Contract Negotiation	Responding to Change over Following a Plan

*Working Software has been replaced with Value
** Working Software has been replaced with Deliverables

Figure 5.5 Agile manifesto

project management delivery method is intended to be coupled with the Agile Manifesto; delivering projects with the Scrum method will be challenging without the foundation of the Agile Manifesto guiding actions and decisions.

Agile project management with the Scrum delivery method is perhaps one of the most popular adaptive project management approaches to develop, deliver, and sustain "complex projects" (Schwaber and Sutherland 2017, 3). A search online will show you other adaptive/agile approaches like Kanban, DevOps, and extreme programming.

While most cybersecurity projects do not need the Scrum agile delivery method (e.g., they usually have low ambiguity levels), the *Shields Up* hybrid project management approach works well when leveraged with the Agile Manifesto's principles and values. There are other project management approaches related to agile project management that we might add to our hybrid project management tool kit: lean project management and Lean Six Sigma.

Lean Project Management

Lean operations and management are recurring themes in the press and this book; we do not want to do more on our projects than necessary. Lean is all about efficiency: doing the right things right. We try to reduce waste in our projects and deliver value for our stakeholders. We include a continuous improvement cycle to become leaner and more effective. Increasingly, many technology projects we implement have lean objectives: for example, we automate business processes to reduce steps for our customers. We should not be surprised that lean principles have been applied to project and information systems management.

Microlearning

Following are some activities to enhance your professional development journey:

- Search for "lean operations" and "lean management" to see what our customers are reading and their expectations to become leaner through technology and automation. IT holds the solution to becoming lean, and cybersecurity specialists protect the lean solution.
- Follow a lean operations or management blog to keep abreast of business trends.

What is lean project management? We use project management methodologies in a way where we reduce waste, delight our customers, and look for improvement opportunities. Lean project management is sometimes mentioned in agile project management as both are somewhat new and compatible techniques. However, lean project management is not another project management methodology like agile or waterfall. Lean project management combines methodologies to create value for the sponsor by optimizing project resources.

Lean Six Sigma

IT professionals interested in best practices discover Lean Six Sigma as another improvement method related to agile project management. Lean

Six Sigma combines lean management and Six Sigma goals (Figure 5.6). Lean Six Sigma aims to improve processes by reducing waste and/or delays and improving quality, resulting in customer satisfaction. Improving processes is attractive to the business since Lean Six Sigma projects can provide three key benefits (Snee 2010, 6):

1. Deliver the maximum value contributing to business goals.
2. Improve process performance for painful steps in the process.
3. Improve information and resource flow while reducing waste and cycle time.

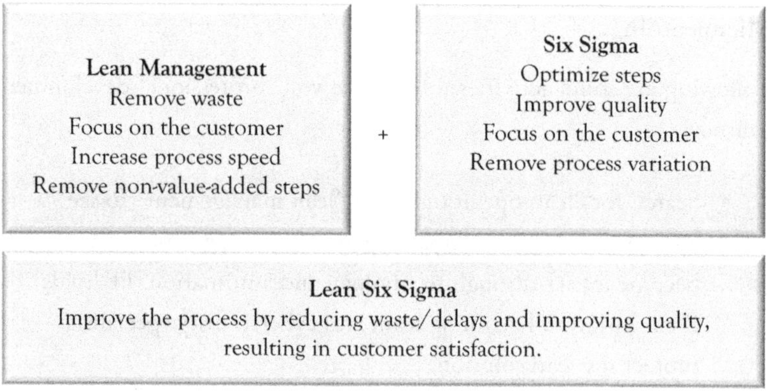

Lean Management
Remove waste
Focus on the customer
Increase process speed
Remove non-value-added steps

+

Six Sigma
Optimize steps
Improve quality
Focus on the customer
Remove process variation

Lean Six Sigma
Improve the process by reducing waste/delays and improving quality, resulting in customer satisfaction.

Figure 5.6 Lean six sigma goals

Exercise

List some of your organization's projects during the last 12 months; how many of them have roots in Lean Six Sigma goals (e.g., optimize steps, remove pain points, and reduce turnaround time)? Many organizations initiate projects to address Lean Six Sigma goals but lack the methods and tools to achieve the desired results!

To gain the benefits of Lean Six Sigma (e.g., to reduce pain points and time to complete the process), users follow the DMAIC process (de Mast and Lokkerbol 2012, 604–614): a data-driven, quality improvement process (Figure 5.7). For example, the business owner (e.g., manufacturing)

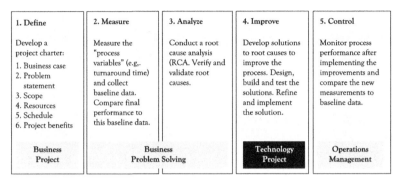

1. Define	2. Measure	3. Analyze	4. Improve	5. Control
Develop a project charter: 1. Business case 2. Problem statement 3. Scope 4. Resources 5. Schedule 6. Project benefits	Measure the "process variables" (e.g,. turnaround time) and collect baseline data. Compare final performance to this baseline data.	Conduct a root cause analysis (RCA. Verify and validate root causes.	Develop solutions to root causes to improve the process. Design, build and test the solutions. Refine and implement the solution.	Monitor process performance after implementing the improvements and compare the new measurements to baseline data.
Business Project	**Business Problem Solving**		**Technology Project**	**Operations Management**

Known as DMAIC (*dee-may-ic*) in Lean Six Sigma vocabulary

Figure 5.7 DMAIC improvement cycle

wants to improve a process (operations) and may follow DMAIC to initiate a quality improvement project. The project team establishes a baseline and measures how long it takes to get through the process targeted for improvement. The project team may interview users of the service to identify process pain points. The business sponsor will then propose a new project to deliver the Lean Six Sigma quality improvement goals. The improvement solution increasingly involves technology to automate steps in a business process with integration, AI, or IoT technologies. Once the solution is delivered and used in business operations, the team remeasures and documents any process improvements. The team resurveys process users to understand the value of quality improvements. IT professionals will see more project requests as part of the *Improve* phase of Lean Six Sigma. Cybersecurity professionals will be invited to join the team to secure the process and data.

Thus, Lean Six Sigma studies by the business are a way IT projects are identified and proposed to the organization. IT subject matter experts (SMEs) might be invited to join Lean Six Sigma projects to (i) implement technologies using a project management delivery approach and (ii) add cybersecurity to the technical solution.

Project Management: Final Thoughts

Project management helps to plan and deliver successful projects. Multiple project delivery approaches range from predictive (traditional waterfall) to adaptive (agile). Traditional project management is often process based, where we initiate a project, plan, design, build, deliver, and closeout the project. The leading project management standards and frameworks follow a similar process, with common theory (e.g., scope, quality, and risk management). One can use a hybrid project management approach (Figure 5.8) to combine elements of different standards and approaches as projects vary by industry (Skulmoski and Brendolan, In Press).

Using a hybrid project management approach, the project manager can become lean in planning and delivering cybersecurity projects. The project manager combines and tailors the right project management-related standards, frameworks, processes, and tools to deliver their cybersecurity projects (Figure 5.8).

Figure 5.8 Cybersecurity hybrid project management

Microlearning

Following are some practical exercises to enhance your learning:

- Search online for Six Sigma free white belt training. Many training organizations offer free online white belt training and certification with the intention the student will sign up for subsequent training (e.g., Six Sigma yellow belt). Within one week of part-time studying the foundations of Lean Six Sigma, one can get a business-oriented certification.
- Which of these frameworks listed in Figure 5.8 are used in your organization? Search online for any unfamiliar frameworks.

PART II

Hybrid Project Management

CHAPTER 6

Cybersecurity Project Management

The purpose of Part 2 is to provide practical guidance to plan and implement cybersecurity projects. This hybrid project management approach originates from theory and standards and has proven best practices for implementing technologies like cybersecurity. The intent is that your adaptation of the *Shields Up* approach will also be lean and tailored to your project's and organization's distinct needs. This hybrid project management approach is aligned with leading project management, ISO 9001 Quality Management, ISO 3100 Risk Management, ITIL, and NIST Frameworks and will help you successfully implement cybersecurity and other technology projects. Indeed, delivering new technical services valued by our organizations depends on effective project management throughout the value chain activities (Limited, AXELOS 2019, 95). Berger et al. (2020, 5) recommended that ITIL 4 "is more than capable" of integrating service management, risk management, ISO 27001 information security management, and the NIST cybersecurity framework. One can bring together the key frameworks to deliver cybersecurity projects (Figure 5.8).

Hybrid Project Management

Hybrid project management combines predictive and adaptive processes (PMI 2021, 100). One uses a hybrid project management approach to adapt to the organizational setting and project; one recognizes that "one size does not fit all."

The 7th Edition of the PMBOK® Guide emphasizes "tailoring" to select the right processes, tools, techniques, and inputs to deliver one's projects (PMI 2021, 131–132). One works from a macro to a micro perspective with a quality improvement cycle (Figure 6.1, after PMI 2021, 137).

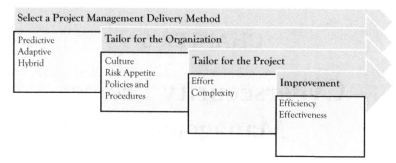

Figure 6.1 *Tailoring your project*

Therefore, hybrid project management allows the project manager to fine-tune the project delivery approach (processes, tools, techniques, and inputs, including personnel) to the organization's needs and project using a tailoring approach.

The first step in the tailoring process is to choose a project management approach; most cybersecurity projects can be implemented using hybrid project delivery (Figure 6.2). Indeed, the ITIL framework is flexible and allows organizations to fine-tune the Service Value Chain to meet the unique demands of their projects (Limited, AXELOS 2019, 18). Most project managers use the traditional project management approach and begin their careers by leading routine or less complex projects with low ambiguity. One predictably progresses through the project phases, primarily when stage gates govern progress. Stage gates (also known as control gates) are decision points where leadership can approve or terminate projects. Stage gates are beneficial if the project manager is new

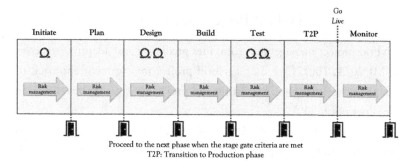

Figure 6.2 *Hybrid project delivery approach*

to managing projects and leadership wants to provide guide rails to help the new project manager successfully deliver their project. Stage gates are improved if they are measurable, objective, and published in advance. For example, we can leave the design phase and enter the build phase if the following documents are approved: (i) application detailed design, (ii) low-level design for infrastructure, and (iii) integration specification. One can also complete a project review at these project inflexion points where project status, project feasibility, and perhaps continued relevancy of the business case are reviewed.

A key benefit of stage gates is poorly performing projects can be terminated or rescued with replanning and approval. Stage gates are widely used to improve rigor, governance, and quality and reduce risk. Stage gates are easy to understand, use, and implement. Include stage gates in your cybersecurity projects to document what you need to deliver, including terminating the project after completing the monitoring period.

Should your organization lack formal stage gates, you can establish stage gates and success criteria with your manager and sponsor. Aligned with the ITIL Service Value Chain, there are milestone documents that the project manager develops, such as an approved project plan that completes the planning phase or the test report that completes the test phase (Table 6.1). In line with lean project management, we minimize the amount of documentation our projects produce; with experience, the quality of our documentation improves and becomes leaner.

The hybrid project delivery approach includes the risk management process (identify, analyze, treat, and control) in each project phase (Figure 6.2). Risk management is critical to delivering successful projects (see the Risk Management section) and underlies most project management efforts and decisions. Finally, the hybrid project delivery approach accommodates iterations when required (Figure 6.2). For example, we might go through an iteration to fine-tune the project scope to initiate the right project. Later, we may face design challenges, especially if the technology we implement is leading edge. We may complete multiple design iteration cycles to finalize the technical design. Likewise, when we test our application, we may encounter defects that require multiple attempts to find a feasible and implementable solution. These iterations may closely

Table 6.1 Stage gate criteria example

	Stage gate criteria
Initiate	Business endorses the project (meeting minutes) Funding is provided (meeting minutes) Feasibility is endorsed (presentation to Change Control Board) Leadership provides approval to proceed (meeting minutes)
Plan	Project Planning Workshop(s) is completed (meeting minutes) Budget is baselined Schedule is baselined Project Planning Document is approved (links to minutes, schedule, and budget)
Design	Design Workshop(s) is completed (minutes) Project Design Document(s) is approved
Build	Build Workshop(s) is completed (meeting minutes) Project Build Document(s) is approved
Test	Test Strategy Document(s) is approved Testing Workshop(s) is completed (meeting minutes) Test Report Document(s) is approved
T2P	T2P Workshop(s) is completed (meeting minutes) T2P Checklist is completed Go Live Plan is approved Change Request is raised
Close Out	Close Out Report is approved Change Control Board approves project closeout Project and team disbandment are documented and archived

or loosely follow the Scrum method (Figure 5.4) depending upon the purpose and capability of the team.

Thus, hybrid project management in *Shields Up* uses the traditional waterfall project management delivery approach, governed by stage gates. The stage gates help govern progress. Underlying progress is risk management and iterative problem-solving cycles. Hybrid project management in *Shields Up* is about combining and tailoring practices, processes, principles, and tools to deliver a successful project. *Shields Up* is aligned with the cybersecurity and project management specialties (Figure 5.8).

When examining the frameworks and standards that guide IT, cybersecurity, and project management activities, one notes they are process-based. They begin with a need or opportunity, and then work is completed, resulting in something of value (Figure 6.3; refer to the original figures for the details. Your eyes are fine!). They address a need

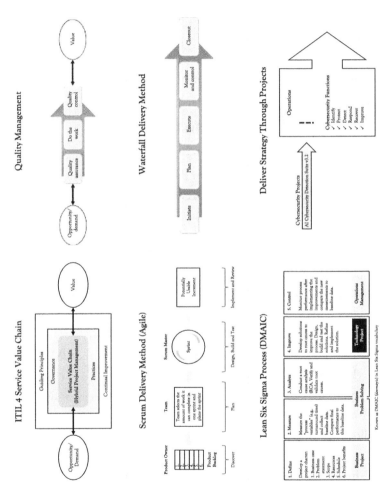

Figure 6.3 Hybrid project management alignment

by converting inputs into outputs by following processes to deliver value to the end user. Project management is the delivery method to provide value in these frameworks and standards. Therefore, your journey to improve your project management capabilities will help you succeed in these other frameworks.

These frameworks and standards begin with the organization identifying a need or opportunity delivered through a project. A process(es) is followed, and value is delivered. Therefore, by following the hybrid project management approach, you align to best practices and processes represented in these international standards and frameworks.

Hybrid Project Management Principles

The hybrid project management principles are intended to guide actions and decisions in most projects, most of the time, including cybersecurity projects (throughout the spectrum of technical to nontechnical projects). These principles help shape project culture and align the team. In project management and technology operations, we interact regularly with new team members both internally and externally. Each new interaction offers the opportunity to bring them into our culture and operational frameworks as we meet needs and opportunities to deliver value to the users of our services. Therefore, as project managers, we can be role models of the principles we value when collaborating with others in projects.

Principles are found in many frameworks such as the PMBOK® Guide, ITIL, PRINCE2, and the Agile Manifesto. These principles are widely applicable and are found in hybrid project management detailed in *Shields Up*. The five hybrid project management principles include the following:

1. **Value orientation**: The reason we work is to deliver value! In cybersecurity projects, we may improve our ability to protect or respond, which our organization values. We take a holistic approach to deliver value and prefer to deliver value early and frequently. We are agile and welcome managed change.
2. **Collaboration**: To deliver value, we regularly collaborate with others to meet expectations and deliver requirements. Our collaborations

build trust through open communication, leading to high-performing teams.

3. **Risk focus**: The key reason we fail to deliver the expected value or meet requirements is that risks occur. Therefore, much of our time is related to managing risks to achieve our plans. When we collaborate with others, we discuss risks either formally or informally, and all decisions are informed to understand risks.

4. **Quality disposition**: Quality management can support risk management. For example, we design-in quality assurance and control into our work to improve the probability of success along the system value chain. We take opportunities to reflect, learn, and optimize ourselves, processes, and technology, reducing future risks.

5. **Engaged leadership**: Leaders act with a sense of urgency and look for opportunities to front-end load. They are customer and value focused. Engaged leaders value inclusiveness and are project management ambassadors.

These hybrid project management principles apply to project managers, sponsors, stakeholders, and both internal and external team members in the value streams.

Hybrid project management allows the team to combine methods and frameworks to tailor their delivery approach to the environment, organization, and project. Tailoring and combining allow a flexible, proactive, and value-focused approach to delivering products and services to the end users. *Shields Up* project management follows a traditional waterfall delivery approach with iterations (agile) to leverage opportunities or solve problems encountered during the design and testing phases (Figure 6.2). Therefore, we begin our projects in the initiation phase when a project is proposed to address an opportunity or need.

CHAPTER 7

Initiate Phase

The hybrid project management project includes an initiation phase (Figure 6.2). Leadership will determine whether the service or product produced by the project (e.g., implementing a new application into the technological ecosystem) is needed. Some projects may include a business plan that justifies the project and outlines its benefits to the organization. Your organization may have a change authorization board that reviews and approves proposed projects. As the project's importance, complexity, and cost increases, so should formality and process rigor. Some organizations use a project initiation document (PID) that includes the following:

1. **Project scope**: a brief description of the work the project will deliver;
2. **Rationale**: an overview of the business case that triggered the project;
3. **Stakeholders**: a brief description of (i) the project team, (ii) those who can impact the project (e.g., sponsor, regulatory bodies, and leadership), and (iii) those who are impacted by the project (e.g., end-users who use the product or service);
4. **Risks and issues**: list the most severe risks and issues;
5. **Project reporting and controls**: include how you will control your project and report progress;
6. **Approval signatures**: some PIDs include the signatures of the sponsors/leadership who have approved project initiation.

You can check with your project management office (PMO) or leadership for project initiation guidance and content if you are responsible for initiating a project. The PID can be energized by making it a one-page infographic. Documenting and illustrating project information on one page becomes a powerful communications tool to use and reuse on your project to orient new stakeholders. Reusing project artifacts contributes to leanness. Supporting the PID is a technical analysis to assure that the organization approves the right project. A professional quality PID is often the first project document a new stakeholder sees and is an early opportunity to demonstrate your professionalism.

Technology Analysis

You might be called upon to assess the proposed technology in a project from a cybersecurity or technical perspective. Perhaps, our business partners have conducted a Lean Six Sigma study, and the process improvement solution is to reduce steps in their process with AI-leveraged automation. When examining a project proposal, assess whether the technology makes sense from a cybersecurity perspective; for example, a business proposal leveraging technology might not be feasible if the cost of securing the new service exceeds the return on investment (Creese et al. 2020, 44). You may discuss the project with your systems architect to ensure that the proposed project "fits" with the system architecture. Suppose the project proposal is a cybersecurity project. In that case, leadership will be interested in how the cybersecurity project will contribute to organizational resilience and growth goals while reducing risk (Scholtz 2021, 4). Many resources guide your technology analysis; instead, we focus on analyzing the technology project from a project management perspective in *Shields Up*.

Exercise

- Develop a well-designed PID template that can be used for subsequent projects. Templates are a way to improve quality and become leaner (see Quality Management).
- Collect for future use project management templates your organization uses to gain a quick start on your project.
- Examine a business case for a project your organization has implemented to understand the contents of a successful business case.
- What are system architecture best practices?
- How to improve system architectures?
- How to align system architectures?

Project Analysis

Selecting the best project depends upon the (i) quality of defined requirements, (ii) quality of the analysis, and (iii) quality of the understanding of what the alternative projects can produce (Daniel, Hempel, and Srinivasan 2001, 39–54). The quality of the requirements comes from the project sponsor (more about project requirements later). You can tactfully challenge the project sponsor about alternative projects: "Help me understand; I am new to this. Can we try this solution instead?" You may need to analyze the project, and the Project Feasibility Gizmo (Skulmoski 2008, 1–6) is a project analysis tool you can use to gain a deep understanding of the project.

Project Feasibility Gizmo

The Project Feasibility Gizmo is a structured method to analyze a proposed project based on the project's complexity and effort required to deliver the project. The Gizmo was developed by project management experts (N = 23) in a three-round Delphi research project. The project effort attributes represent the degree of complexity to deliver the project (e.g., type of work, communications, scope integration, and uncertainty and risk of the project environment. The project contextual complexity attributes are external to a project and include constraints, uncertainty, and risk in the external environment; relative project size; project criticality; and the business environment (Skulmoski 2008, 2). One can assess the project by its complexity attributes and the anticipated effort to complete the project. Using the Project Feasibility Gizmo, the project manager can quickly complete a comprehensive project assessment that can strengthen the technical analysis of your project or a project you have been asked to assess. (See Appendix 2 for the Project Feasibility Gizmo and instructions for use.)

When completing a feasibility assessment with the Gizmo, one develops a deeper appreciation of the project attributes to help you tailor and manage your project. We begin by examining the six project complexity attributes that will impact your project and will help you to tailor your project:

1. **Constraints**: The project manager will likely face some constraints that can impact the quality of the product or service you deliver and challenge meeting budget and schedule targets.
2. **Relative project size**: The size of the project will impact how you manage your project: larger projects often face more governance and increased formality than smaller ones.
3. **Project criticality**: Projects are prioritized, and the degree of project criticality relates to the amount of governance and formality required to manage your project. Early career project managers usually are assigned less critical projects. Understanding project criticality to your sponsor also contributes to improved project alignment.
4. **Uncertainty and risk (external)**: All projects face uncertainty and risk; they impact the project and how the project manager organizes work. Projects that are highly uncertain with many risks are more challenging to manage and may require a larger team and more formality. Even projects with less uncertainty and fewer risks can benefit from a formal risk management approach—the secret to project success!
5. **Organizational environment**: We do not manage projects in a vacuum; the culture and governance impact how we manage our projects.
6. **Business environment**: The projects we manage are impacted by the external business environment. For example, working with a global team can add to project complexity.

Understanding the complexity of your project sooner rather than later improves the odds of project success. By assessing each attribute with the Gizmo, you methodically evaluate project complexity. The Project Feasibility Gizmo helps us appreciate the contextual complexity of project attributes external to the project. For example, the same project in Helsinki will likely be managed differently in Abu Dhabi or Moose Jaw due to the different external project environments. Understanding the external environment early in the project allows us to identify risks and issues when they are easiest to manage.

Next, we assess the effort required to deliver the project. We use the Gizmo to examine project effort attributes:

1. **Type of work**: The first project effort attribute is the type of work we are doing: building a bridge over a river, conducting a NIST compliance audit, or adding new security event management software. Some projects require more and different types of effort the project manager needs to understand when planning a project. For example, are we implementing only the basic functionality, or is the project innovative (e.g., early adoption of technology)? Whatever our first projects may be, they will probably be relatively smaller, less complex, and less critical to the organization, with a greater degree of latitude to drift from approved project targets.

2. **Communications**: The nature of the communications impacts our project and the type of risks and issues we must manage. For example, auditing often involves gathering data from others, such as our colleagues in the PMO and Infrastructure teams who might not be in the same building as us, while upgrading a backup tool will require fewer communications. Therefore, the number of stakeholders and their location affects our projects.

3. **Integration scope**: The number of different project elements that need to be integrated affects our project effort; the more elements to integrate (e.g., budget and schedule reports, status reports, external stakeholders, human resource management, and contract management), the more significant effort is required to complete the project successfully. Integration scope can be a significant source of risks and issues discovered using the Gizmo.

4. **Uncertainty and risk (internal)**: The complexity of the effort, the type of work, the number of project elements that need to be integrated, and so on all bring risks and issues that the project manager manages. Less complex projects that require less effort are often the first types of projects assigned to new project managers.

The output of using the Project Feasibility Gizmo is the project manager has systematically gathered valuable project information with which to plan and to prevent risks from becoming issues—the Achilles Heel of technology projects. The project manager is encouraged to repeat the exercise with the project sponsor and their SME team if there is more than average uncertainty (e.g., a range of possible outcomes). You could find that you and the sponsor have very different perspectives of the project feasibility attributes resulting in misalignment at the beginning of the project; misalignment is not uncommon and working through the Gizmo brings alignment.

Exercise

Assess a project you have under consideration or one where you were a team member. Use the Project Feasibility Assessment Gizmo included in Appendix 2.

A key benefit from using the Project Feasibility Gizmo is that you address the Ability to Change Paradox directly and early in the project, thereby improving your probability of project success.

The Ability to Change Paradox

The Ability to Change Paradox (Figure 7.1) faces all project managers and can affect project success if not properly managed (Hartman 1999a, np). At the start of the project, one has very little information about the project. However, the amount of information we have increased throughout the project (e.g., we know which risks became issues, which project personnel delivered consistently on time, and which procurement delays were unavoidable). Over time, our ability to make changes decreases; it is easy to add scope or change the testing approach in the first week of the project compared to the later stages (e.g., changing design when testing is finishing up is difficult). And if we wish to make changes, they are less costly to make at the beginning of the project than during later phases. Therefore, during the initiating and planning phases, our analysis can shift the information curve if we leverage the opportunity provided by the Ability to Change Paradox, work with the right stakeholders, and follow the hybrid project management processes and principles.

Ability to Change Paradox: When changes are least costly and easiest to make at the beginning of the project, we lack information; however, when we have better information later in the project, those changes are often complicated and expensive.

If risks are discovered later in the project, they may become issues resulting in a less than successful project with issues like missed milestones, overbudget expenditures, and quality compromises. We can mitigate this problem by shifting the information curve: bringing forward information (Figure 7.1) to increase the quality and quantity of information sooner rather than later in the project. The Project Feasibility Gizmo is a tool that guides the project manager to understand the project better sooner, thereby shifting the information curve. The project manager learns more about the project to develop better plans, with greater lead time to manage project risks and avoid costly changes later; the foundation of front-end loading.

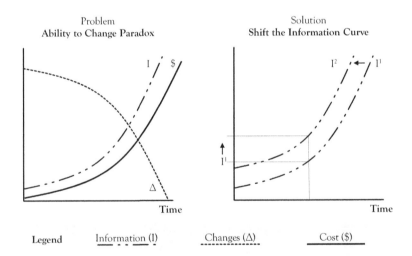

Figure 7.1 Ability to change paradox

Initiate Phase: Final Thoughts

During the initiation phase, the project manager strives to get formal approval to initiate the project. The project manager works with the project sponsor to develop a PID that gives authority to the project manager to proceed to the planning phase. The Gizmo might be used to develop a deeper understanding of the project to shift the information curve to avoid costly changes later in the project.

Microlearning

Following are some online learning activities to deepen your understanding of the initiate phase; search for:

- How to create an infographic?
- What KPIs are used in project management? Planning and using project management KPIs and project assessment criteria can help you deliver the right amount of project management quality.
- How does the ITIL 4 change control practice work?

Examine your organization:

- Identify the project management KPIs your organization tracks and reports. Are these the best KPIs to measure progress?
- Investigate how your organization initiates projects.

CHAPTER 8

Plan Phase

The purpose of the planning phase is to develop a plan that defines and *predicts* how the project will be executed, how much the project will cost, when the work will be executed and completed, the risks and issues encountered, and so on. The project manager identifies the work to be completed and who will complete the work. The project manager will produce a plan that expands the PID and may include a detailed schedule and budget. The goal is to approve the project plan to exit the planning phase.

Lean Project Planning Process

Lean project planning focuses on reducing waste and satisfying our stakeholders. We can follow a lean project planning process (Figure 8.1) to expeditiously plan and shift the information curve resulting in better project plans. This phase aims to develop a lean project plan for leadership approval. We begin the process by meeting with our project sponsor and begin planning:

1. **Mission statement:** Validate the mission statement (scope statement) developed with the sponsor and make it measurable and objective. (e.g., complete an audit of all IT services by June 2023; there is no budget as this is an internal project.)
2. **Project priority:** Identify the project priority (Priority Triangle, discussed later) to achieve alignment.
3. **Success criteria:** Document project success criteria (Done–Won–Who, discussed later) which also contribute to alignment.
4. **Work breakdown structure:** Use the mission statement to develop a high-level work breakdown structure (WBS) that identifies the main work packages.

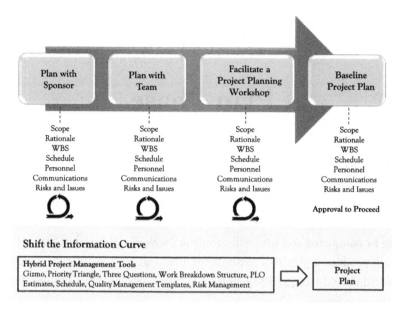

Figure 8.1 Hybrid project planning process

5. **Schedule:** Use the WBS to develop a high-level Gantt chart (bar chart), and if your project is sufficiently large, develop a schedule detailing the critical path and float. Smaller projects can often be managed with a task list and completion dates aligned with the Gantt chart.

6. **Budget:** Some projects do not require a budget as they are internal projects requiring minimal external resources. However, some projects require significant external resources (e.g., technical expertise and new equipment) to complete and benefit from following project budget and cost management processes.

7. **Risks and issues:** Identify critical risks and issues (I always include the message "our project can fail, but with your support, we are more likely to succeed!" to encourage buy-in from the sponsor).

8. **Governance:** Agree on governance and reporting (e.g., What information does the project sponsor and other stakeholders desire? Will there be monthly or weekly status meetings?).

9. **Project roles and responsibilities:** Agree on the project sponsor and project manager.

10. **Lessons learned:** Conduct a lessons learned exercise at the start of your project. Ask the sponsor about what went well and what was challenging on previous projects, so you can benefit from the lessons learned at the start of the project. Your sponsor will appreciate your willingness to incorporate their ideas into your project; you have started effective team building.

Next, after planning with the project sponsor, meet with the SMEs to complete the work identified in the WBS. We repeat much of what we have completed with the project sponsor: review the mission statement and project priority (we can use the PID infographic to begin planning meetings). We examine the WBS to see if anything is missing. Thus, we have an iterative and inclusive approach to project planning, beginning with the project sponsor and main project contributors.

We take an iterative and inclusive approach to develop the project plan. We begin planning with the sponsor and key project participants. We develop a high-level project plan to be presented to key stakeholders in a project planning workshop (PPW) (see Project Planning Workshop section). Additional feedback is gathered in the workshop, and the team endorses the project plan. The plan is then presented to leadership for approval (e.g., baseline the project plan).

Microlearning

In *Shields Up*, we use many traditional project management tools and processes (e.g., budgeting and scheduling) because they have a long history of success. Therefore, we direct the students to search online to improve their understanding of the essential project management tools and processes. You can search online for detailed instructions and templates to complete the following components of a project plan.

- How to create a project charter?
- How to write a project mission statement?
- How to create a WBS?
- How to create a Gantt chart?
- How to create a project network diagram?

- How to create a project budget?
- How to create a RACI chart?
- How to manage version control?
- How to sell anything?
- How to tell a great story?
- How to create a design and layout?

Since baselining the project plan involves gaining the trust of your team, you might consider any approval process in the project life cycle to be a selling exercise. Therefore, "how to sell anything" and "storytelling" are added since they are powerful techniques to help you get approval to proceed. Design and layout considerations, graphics, and other creative considerations will give your project plan a professional look. You are likely to use selling, storytelling, layout, and design skills throughout your career.

While *Shields Up* is more strategically focused, we include project management tools and methods that are lesser known but effective. These tools help us shift the information curve to learn more about your project sooner rather than later when changes are challenging to make and expensive.

Priority Triangle

Project alignment is an early goal project managers work toward since it helps to shift the information curve for the project team. Misalignment increases risks and issues like scope creep, delays, and cost overruns. However, when the project team is aligned, the team is more likely to become lean, and project success is more likely. We saw that the Project Feasibility Gizmo helps shift the information curve; the Gizmo also aligns the project team. The Priority Triangle (Skulmoski and Hartman 2000, 33–37) is another project management tool contributing to team alignment and risk reduction.

The Priority Triangle (Figure 8.2) is adapted from Martin Barnes classical iron triangle, also known as the triple constraint theory (Kerzner 2013, 869). Project teams are constrained by scope, time, cost, and

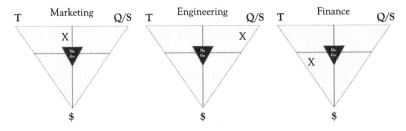

Legend: T=Time, $=Cost, Q=Quality, S=Scope
faster, better, cheaper; choose two

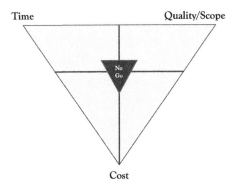

Figure 8.2 Priority triangle and alignment

quality; a change in one constraint will affect the others. For example, if our client asks to increase the scope, we may face increased costs and schedule overruns due to the extra work to deliver the increased scope.

In practice, we can use the triple constraint theory to help identify the project priority. We begin by drawing the Priority Triangle (Skulmoski and Hartman 2000, 35). Time is shown to the left of the Priority Triangle since we wish to minimize the duration of our project. Cost is at the bottom of the Priority Triangle because we try to minimize costs. Finally, quality and scope are to the right since we wish to optimize scope and quality. We try to minimize delivery time; therefore, time is to the left (earlier rather than later) on the Priority Triangle. We wish to maximize value; therefore, quality and scope are to the right on the Priority Triangle.

However, if we ask the project sponsor to identify the priority, the project sponsor will likely choose all constraints as the priority. Therefore, we have added a *No-Go* zone in the middle to force project stakeholders to identify the two most essential project priorities.

Let's look at the Priority Triangle in use. Our project is to add collaborative robots to a manufacturing process. We have three main stakeholders for our IT automation project: marketing, engineering, and finance (Figure 8.2). We explain the exercise, and marketing places their X in the triangle to indicate that delivering on time is the project priority, with quality and scope being the second priority. Their rationale is that marketing wants to start selling the product the project will produce. They also desire high quality since quality products are easier to sell. Engineering has prioritized quality since high-quality components are easier to maintain and have less frequent breakdowns. Finance prioritizes finishing according to budget, followed by finishing on schedule. Finance is responsible for maximizing the use of resources and therefore supports finishing according to the approved budget. They also want to finish on time to generate revenue once the collaborative robot automation is operational.

You can see that the three stakeholders are misaligned with different project priorities (Figure 8.2). We become aligned by getting project priority direction from the project sponsor using the Priority Triangle. In this case, let us assume that finishing on time with the right quality/scope are the sponsor's two project priorities. The project manager has flexibility over the budget to deliver the other two priorities.

In practice, to deliver on time, the project manager may allow his team to work overtime to meet project milestones, even though working overtime may increase costs. However, to deliver on time, the right scope, and to the right level of quality, the project manager has the authority to overspend (within reason). The project team will know it is OK to work overtime to meet the schedule. The project manager knows the team is working overtime since he follows best practices and is close to his team (e.g., PMBOK® Guide principle: engage your stakeholders). The project manager will raise a risk if there is a probability they will overspend, and an issue if there is overspending. The project manager regularly informs status to the sponsor of the project, especially if risks are becoming issues (see Risk Management).

The project manager documents the priority in the project plan, including its implications (e.g., the budget may be exceeded). However, the project manager will work to meet budget, quality, scope and schedule targets with proper risk management. After establishing the project priority, check it throughout the project to determine if the priority has changed. Determining the project priority helps to shift the information curve and reduce risks and issues.

Success Criteria: Done–Won–Who

There are three questions we can ask stakeholders to establish and maintain project alignment (Skulmoski and Hartman 2000, 34–35):

1. **Done**: When is the project finished for you? Most projects have staggered finish dates due to the nature of the work delivered. For example, our procurement team might be finished our project once servers are delivered and tested. However, the project is not finished for cybersecurity until the application goes live and cybersecurity functionality is operationalized and stabilized. The project manager needs to understand a team with different completion dates; otherwise, teams may depart the project sooner than expected.
2. **Won**: What must be delivered for you to be delighted? Define project success and make it measurable and objective. For example, the penetration testing team would like two weeks' notice for their testing services; too often, they are asked to participate in last-minute testing that throws them off their schedule.
3. **Who**: Who gets to vote on the first two questions? We identify the key stakeholders: those who can impact our project and those impacted by our project. We engage these stakeholders early in the project to reduce changes later due to not consulting with a critical project stakeholder.

Again, the three-question tool helps shift the information curve as we better understand the project completion dates and success criteria early in our project.

Exercise

- For an existing or past project that you worked on, what was the project priority? Was there team alignment? Did project priority change during the project?
- For an existing or past project that you worked on, complete a Done–Won–Who exercise. Did the project plan reflect the success criteria from asking when the project is done? What must be delivered for the project to be successful? Who gets to vote on the first two questions?

Project Schedule

Some believe one of the most important documents a project manager creates is a project schedule, and you are likely expected to create a schedule for your project. There are two common forms of schedule: a Gantt chart and a network diagram (Figure 8.3). You might not be able to read the details easily; instead, the purpose of the illustration is to display the conceptual relationship between the mission statement, WBS, Gantt chart, and network diagram. The Gantt chart is a bar chart that we derive from our WBS. The Gantt chart is the type of schedule typically shown to leadership since it clearly shows the start and finish dates for each phase, milestones, and the overall project completion date.

The network diagram illustrates the start and finish of project activities, their logical dependencies, and who is responsible for task completion. For example, the network diagram illustrates the logic to procure servers before configuring, testing, and provisioning servers. The project team uses the network diagram to find the most efficient way to organize the project. The network diagram is tactical and can be developed in a scheduling application. The network diagram allows in-depth analysis to identify the critical path (the longest path through the network) and understand slack (also known as float and is the amount of time a task can be delayed without impacting other dependent tasks).

The project manager collaborates with stakeholders to develop a Gantt chart and network diagram. Often, a high-level Gantt chart is presented

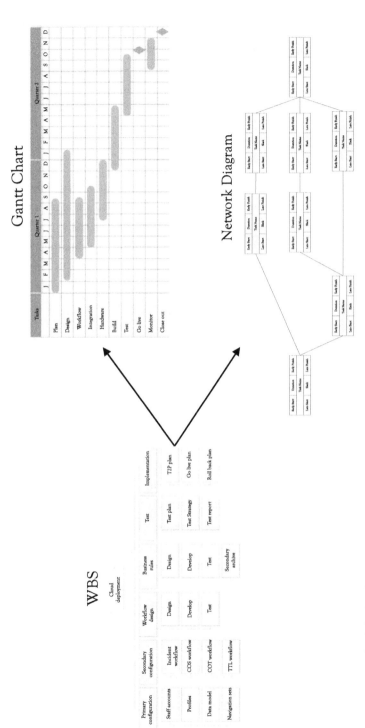

Figure 8.3 Schedule development

in the main body of the project plan to give an overview of the schedule. At the same time, the detailed network diagram is included in the project plan appendixes, with a link to the complete project schedule. To develop these schedules, the project manager asks the most dreaded question to the SMEs: "how long will it take?"

Three-Point Estimating

All schedules are developed with activity duration estimates; some estimates are top-down, where a sponsor gives the project manager a target completion date. Top-down estimates can be very aggressive and challenging to meet. Another way to estimate is bottom-up estimating; we use the WBS and estimate the duration each work package takes to complete, add up the durations, and arrive at the required effort. We then apply these estimates to our network diagram to determine the critical path and slack.

The most common way of estimating is to use single-point estimates; for example, 25 days, $25,000, 8 consultants, and 60 hours. Project managers often ask SMEs how long it will take to complete application testing. The SME is required to give one number, such as three weeks. However, what if the SME encounters more than average defects and the resolution time for some take longer than average? What if technical support from the vendor to fix the defects is delayed? What if testing goes perfectly, there are minimal defects, and we finish earlier than anticipated? The testing SME does not want to give a number too low or too high but does not have a way to communicate estimate uncertainty. Often, the SMEs delay responding to the project manager because they do not know which number to give. For complex, risky, and ambiguous projects, gathering estimates from a team of SMEs can take months. There is a better way: three-point estimates (also known as PLOs: perfect, likely, and outrageous conditions of uncertainty).

Three-point estimates have their origins in classical program evaluation review technique (PERT) scheduling theory. PERT provides a way to calculate how much time it will take to complete the project. PERT calculations capture duration estimates under three different conditions: (i) optimistic (the quickest time to complete a task), (ii) pessimistic (the maximum time to complete a task), and (iii) most likely (the time between the maximum and minimum times—some risks occur, but you also have some luck). We use a weighted average formula to generate a calculated estimate based on statistics.

In *Shields Up,* we apply a modified PERT estimating technique pioneered by Professor Francis Hartman known as PLO estimating (1999b, np). The first improvement is that the terminology has changed; rather than optimistic, we use perfect, and rather than pessimistic, we use outrageous. The name changes intend to better understand the "tail ends" of the normal distribution curve where extreme and compound risks and opportunities exist. Often when risks become issues, a chain reaction occurs where a delay can trigger other risks and issues, resulting in a snowball effect of trouble for the project. When a perfect estimate is received, we challenge to see if we can improve the estimate; for example, we may ask if the time can be improved if they receive help? Or can the time be improved if the vendor configures the server onsite rather than the SME? We look for a scenario where everything goes right, we have lots of luck, and we are promoted at the end of the project! We bring creativity and innovation into the process to complete the activity we are estimating. By examining ways to optimize the time, we find opportunities in the schedule.

We take a similar approach in outrageous estimates; we examine the tail end of risks becoming issues and triggering other risks and issues. For example, we need to estimate how long it will take to complete testing. We may receive an outrageous estimate and ask if the estimate includes the vendor being away sick.[1] We again challenge whether a defect may be resolved only with a future patch resulting in an additional increase to the outrageous estimate. We set up the outrageous scenario where many activities face issues. Therefore, we can capture estimates that include compound and complex risks and opportunities by using outrageous and perfect.

---

[1] I lead a project where the European vendor closed his office for a month in December and January when 75% of his company (18 people in total) were sick with the Flu. The owner looked after his team and shut down the company for a month to help everyone recover. Our vendor returned to the project in mid-January, and our project was delayed three weeks. We rebaselined our project schedule using the change control process.

We set up our spreadsheet to reflect the three conditions of uncertainty: perfect, likely, and outrageous (Figure 8.4). We follow the WBS to estimate the time to complete each work package. We meet with each project team to capture their duration estimates (meeting face-to-face or online to determine duration estimates rather than through e-mails aligns with the principles of the Agile Manifesto and the PMBOK® Guide v7). We capture the likely, perfect, and outrageous estimates and then show the SME the calculated and likely estimates. We next discuss risk and wide-range estimates.

Activity	Likely
A	20
B	20
C	15
D	30
E	20
Total days	105.0

Activity	Calc estimate	Perfect	Likely	Outrageous
A	28.5	6	20	85
B	20.0	16	20	24
C	22.8	11	15	66
D	35.8	5	30	90
E	20.0	18	20	22
Total days	127.2	56.0	105.0	287.0

A) Begin by estimating the likely estimate. Which is the most risky activity?

B) Wide-range estimates inform us of risky activities (Activities A, C and D), and opportunities to crash (Activities A and D).

$$\text{Calculated Estimate} = \frac{(P+4L+O)}{6}$$

Figure 8.4 PLO estimates

Wide-range estimates illustrate risks that activities will take longer than planned and opportunities to reduce the time to complete activities through crashing. The critical point is that you and your team members have identified risks and opportunities; risk/opportunity identification is the first step in risk management. We use simple qualitative risk management techniques for all the wide-range estimates to quickly analyze and establish plans to manage these wide-range risks and opportunities (see Risk Management).

Thus, within 30 to 60 minutes, we can capture duration estimates from a stakeholder. We start with a project overview using the project charter infographic that includes the project priority. We capture the estimates for three conditions of uncertainty (perfect, likely, and outrageous), identify, analyze, and treat risks. We document the risk management plan for wide-range estimates in the risk register and move to the next SME to repeat the PLO exercise.

a) Gather duration estimates by phase

PMO	Calc Estimate	Perfect	Likely	Outrageous
Plan	107.0	35	88	255
Design	63.0	24	58	122
Build	44.8	30	46	55
Test	83.0	26	58	240
Roll Out	67.0	40	65	102
Close Out	21.0	10	20	36
Total Hours	385.8	165.0	335.0	810.0

b) Summarize PLOs by project team (internal use)

Team	Calc Estimate	Perfect	Likely	Outrageous
PMO	385.8	165.0	335.0	810.0
MIS	335.8	105.0	292.0	742.0
Finance	132.8	40.0	96.0	373.0
ESB	175.3	53.0	134.0	463.0
Security	228.5	80.0	172.0	603.0
Infrastructure	143.7	45.0	115.0	357.0
Total Hours	1,402.0	488.0	1,144.0	3,348.0

c) Summarize PLOs by project team and phase for leadership
d) Use the Calculated Estimate values since most readers are unfamiliar with the PLO estimating method

Team	Plan	Design	Build	Test	Monitor	Close Out	Total	% of Total
PMO	107	63	45	83	67	21	385.8	28%
MIS	13	102	59	88	73	2	335.8	24%
Finance	13	16	10	59	33	2	132.8	9%
ESB	14	28	53	49	29	2	175.3	13%
Security	13	73	39	65	37	2	228.5	16%
Infrastructure	9	34	32	33	34	2	143.7	10%
Total Hours	168	316	238	377	273	31	1,402.0	100%

Figure 8.5 Summarized PLO duration estimates

Once we capture the estimates from all contributing SMEs (Figure 8.5a), we are ready to summarize and analyze the results (Figure 8.5b). When we summarize PLOs by the project team (or WBS work package), we can see which teams face the most risk: wide-range estimates (Figure 8.5b). We further arrange the data to illustrate PLOs by team and project phase to understand better the effort required for each phase (Figure 8.5d). We display the calculated estimate rather than PLOs since the reader/approver is unlikely to be familiar with this technique. However, they welcome single-point estimates; the calculated estimates appear like single-point estimates and will not take the attention away from your estimates to a discussion about an innovative estimating technique (PLO estimating). Therefore, use the calculated duration estimates when you develop your schedules.

The benefits of using PLOs and the risk management process are they shift the information curve more than any other technique in the planning phase. Not only have we quickly captured duration estimates, but we also understand the risks and the opportunities to crash if we begin to fall behind our schedule. Few other project tools can deepen our understanding of the project early in the project life cycle as PLO estimates with risk management.

Using PLOs (three-point estimates) provides many benefits, as hinted previously:

1. **Fast estimates**: We saw the challenge single-point estimates give to SMEs where single-point estimates do not easily account for uncertainty. PLOs provide three conditions of uncertainty which makes it easier to provide high-quality estimates. It takes only half an hour to capture estimates from an SME for most projects. In one week of face-to-face meetings, the project manager can complete the first round of risk-informed estimating. It is common to show the SMEs the completed draft to see if anything was missed or if the estimates should be revised.

2. **Risk-sensitive estimates**: The estimates account for risks and opportunities; therefore, the PLO estimates are more realistic than most single-point estimates. Even when single-point estimates are used and a 10 percent contingency is added, we may still be underestimating. For example, the likely estimate total is 105 days, while

the calculated estimate is 127.2 days (Figure 8.4). If we used the likely and added a contingency (105 + 10.5 = 115.5), we would still be almost 12 days under the calculated estimate. When you search online for "IT project success rate" and look at the percentage of IT projects that finish on time, you will find that around half of all IT projects are late; that is, the project needed more time than was approved. Perhaps, if the project manager followed the three-point estimating method and used calculated estimates in the schedule, many of these IT projects would have finished on time using more realistic PLO estimates.

3. **Risks are identified**: It becomes evident where risks exist by looking at wide-range estimates (Figure 8.4 and Figure 8.5b). For example, activities A, C, and D have wide ranges between the likely and outrageous estimates; if the risks are not properly managed, these three activities could take much longer to complete than the likely estimate. We have identified three risky activities, and the project manager and SME can make plans to prevent and mitigate the associated risks. Not only have we quickly captured duration estimates, but we also know where key risks exist and how to treat them. Without PLOs, single-point estimates might mislead us to where our risks exist. For example, in Figure 8.4, if asked which is the riskiest activity, many people would guess activity D since it has the largest duration (30 days). However, activities A and C are risky but might not have been identified as risky activities using single-point estimates since their duration estimates are relatively low. PLOs help us find and prioritize risks.

4. **Opportunities are identified**: When we use PLOs, we can identify opportunities to crash activities should we fall behind and wish to make up time. For example, in Figure 8.4, if we need to crash activities to catch up, we will choose activities A and D to crash (e.g., they are on the critical path) due to the wide range between the perfect and likely estimates. We would not want to prioritize activities B, C, and E to crash since there is little time to gain by crashing.

5. **Improved estimate quality**: Since the estimating technique is methodical and estimates include risks and issues, our PLO estimates are better than single-point estimates. With PLO estimates, the project manager understands each estimate's risks and opporttu-

nities, develops risk and issue management plans, and records them in the risk register. The PLO estimating technique helps shift the information curve resulting in better quality estimates and improved schedule success.

6. **Enhanced professionalism**: When you efficiently complete the estimating process, have identified risks and opportunities, and have a risk management plan, your standing with your peers and leadership will be enhanced. Using the PLO method is a career booster since you shift the information curve by understanding risks, issues, and opportunities and improving project success with risk management.

Now that we have duration estimates, we use these calculated estimates to develop our schedule. We add the logic of predecessors and successors and assign people to each task. Scheduling programs can then provide us with a detailed schedule to baseline. The calculated duration estimates are also used to update the Gantt chart. Now that scheduling is completed, we develop our budget.

Exercise

Set up a spreadsheet template to capture PLO estimates by phase for multiple contributing teams for use in future projects.

Project Budget

Budgeting follows a similar process to schedule; rather than asking "how long will it take," ask "how much will it cost," and use the PLO estimating technique to derive the calculated estimate for our budget. As noted earlier, some projects do not require a budget since the resources are internal and no external expenses are required (e.g., consultants or new hardware). Suppose your project requires a more sophisticated approach (e.g., you need to determine indirect and overhead costs). In that case, finance and procurement SMEs can guide you to develop a budget in-line with your organization's budget procedures.

However, we can follow the WBS to guide our estimates and develop the project budget (Figure 8.6). Our WBS illustrates our project scope;

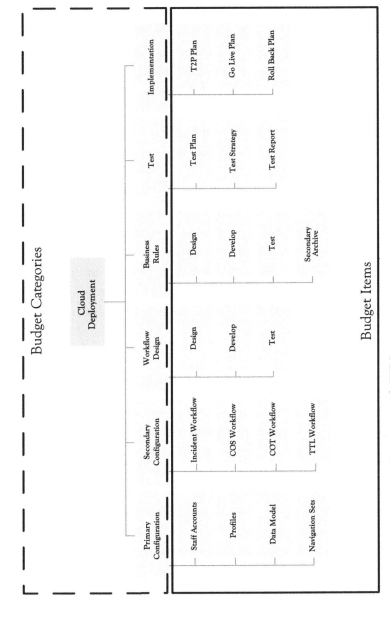

Figure 8.6 Budget development with WBS

therefore, we can develop a "bottom-up" budget with our WBS. The top part of a WBS has the budget categories (e.g., Workflow Design), and the bottom contains the activities. We estimate the cost of the activities and "roll them up" into our budget categories. We show leadership a budget based on the categories (high-level) rather than the detailed budget based on budget items. We can include the high-level budget in the main body of the project plan and a more detailed budget in the project plan's appendix if the reader requires more information. (We can use the same approach in the schedule, where we can show leadership a Gantt chart based on the top portion of the WBS: Primary Configuration through to Implementation. We use the bottom activities as the basis of our network diagram.)

We can capture cost estimates similarly to schedule estimates when we meet with the most capable SME to provide cost estimates. Begin by reviewing the project charter, Priority Triangle, and PLO estimating method. We capture the estimates for perfect, likely, and outrageous conditions of uncertainty. We use the calculated estimates in the detailed and high-level budgets. We complete the budget exercise by looking for wide-range estimates, identifying risks, and updating our risk register for budget-related risks and issues.

Project Communications

A lean approach to project management is to consider project human resources and communications management at the same time since our communications focus on people. Human resources management is the process of leading, coordinating, and managing the project team and determining your team's roles and responsibilities. Project communications management involves ensuring that the right people receive the right project information at the right time. Effective communications do not just happen; they need to be planned, managed, and monitored. There are many forms of project communication like e-mails, risk registers, schedules, budgets, status reports, and application design documents; many of these forms of communication result from project meetings.

Projects are collaborative efforts often supported with meetings to progress execution (Table 8.1). Meetings can be in a workshop format

Table 8.1 Monthly project meeting schedule

Monday	Tuesday	Wednesday	Thursday	Friday
1. You have two projects: Projects 1 and 2, and you meet with your teams using stand up meetings 2. Each week you prepare for a status meeting with your director by meeting with your team lead 3. The team reviews risks and issues on a weekly basis 4. Each month you and other project managers provide status updates to your CIO/CISO at an Executive Leadership Meeting				1 Stand Up Project 1 Director Project Review
4 Stand Up Project 1	5 Stand Up Project 1 Stand Up Project 2 Risk and Issues Review	6 Stand Up Project 1 Team Lead prepares Status Report	7 Stand Up Project 1 Project Manager Status Review	8 Stand Up Project 1 Director Project Review
11 Stand Up Project 1	12 Stand Up Project 1 Stand Up Project 2 Risk and Issues Review	13 Stand Up Project 1 Team Lead prepares Status Report	14 Stand Up Project 1 Project Manager Status Review	15 Stand Up Project 1 Director Project Review
18 Stand Up Project 1	19 Stand Up Project 1 Stand Up Project 2 Risk and Issues Review	20 Stand Up Project 1 Team Lead prepares Status Report	21 Stand Up Project 1 Project Manager Status Review Director Project Review	22 Stand Up Project 1 Director Project Review Executive Leadership Review
25 Stand Up Project 1	26 Stand Up Project 1 Stand Up Project 2 Risk and Issues Review	27 Stand Up Project 1 Team Lead prepares Status Report	28 Stand Up Project 1 Project Manager Status Review	29 Stand Up Project 1 Director Project Review

to develop a schedule, document the design, and test the product. The project manager sets up workshops according to the project schedule. The project manager also sets up recurring meetings to support the communication process with status reports to leadership as part of their governance role. In this example of a monthly project meeting schedule, the focus is to report to the project director weekly and executive leadership for a monthly project review. The schedule allows the project manager and team to meet throughout the week in standup meetings to plan the project activities for the day. There is also a weekly risk management meeting. These daily standups and risk management meetings help the project manager monitor and control project activities and relate the project status to leadership. The project manager needs to set up a similar meeting and communications schedule to support project activities. Often, a key challenge is to find a meeting space if the meetings are face-to-face. Setting up the meeting schedule and booking the meeting rooms is a project activity that can be front-end loaded; teams appreciate meetings that recur in the same room, which can be achieved with early scheduling.

Discuss with your leadership the information they require in project status reports. Status reports can be improved if they are aligned with the project priority; if the priority is on time and cost, then the status report will have schedule and budget information and the related risks and issues.

Many project managers develop a RACI chart (sometimes called a responsibility matrix) to help manage communications by clarifying roles and responsibilities for critical tasks and milestones (Table 8.2). Projects that lack a RACI chart face the risks of role confusion and omitting people in the communications process. The project manager assigns four different roles to project participants to improve communication and coordination:

1. **Responsible:** The person(s) who will complete the task. While multiple people can be assigned responsibility to complete a task, too many Rs can congest and delay the activity (e.g., "too many cooks in the kitchen").

2. **Accountable:** The person responsible for delegating and overseeing the completion of the task (task owner) but might not be doing the

work. There should only be one person accountable for each task and milestone. The accountable person usually approves the work completed by the responsible SME.

3. **Consulted:** The person who may provide expert advice (two-way communication). Project managers try to balance who needs to be consulted since too many Cs can delay a project.

4. **Informed:** People who need to know about the activity progress but are not directly involved in the work; they are given high-level rather than detailed project information (one-way communication).

The project manager will analyze the RACI chart to ensure no empty cells and that no SME is overburdened with work (too many Rs). The project manager discusses the assigned roles with the team to get their buy-in. Once the RACI chart is completed with a high-level communications, plan is completed.

Table 8.2 RACI chart

Task/milestone	Project manager	Project sponsor	SME #1	SME #2	SME #3
Activity A	A	I	R	C	I
Milestone 1	A	C	C	R	I
Activity B	A	I	R	I	C
Activity C	A	I	C	C	R
Milestone 2	A	C	I	C	R

Risk Management

Risk management is a critical success factor for technology projects and is a recommended ITIL general management practice (Limited, AXELOS 2019, 95–97); get risk management right, and the probability of project success exponentially increases. Risk management in *Shields Up* is aligned with ISO 31000:2018 Risk management—Guidelines (ISO 2018b);

therefore, when you follow risk management in *Shields Up,* you are aligned with ISO 27000 Risk Management. Lean risk management centers on the risk management process supported by a risk register, quality management, and simple techniques that can be used on most projects, most of the time. Risk management is the process of planning, identifying, analyzing, treating, and controlling risks and issues. Risks and issues may be negative (e.g., delays) or positive (e.g., opportunities to crash an activity) and can be managed with the risk management process and risk register.

The risk management process (Figure 8.7) is simple and effective; you can use this approach on most projects, most of the time. All project plans should include a section about risk and issue management. The project manager provides an overview of how risks and issues will be managed and communicated, the tools and processes used, and so on. For example, the project manager may schedule weekly risk management meetings (Table 8.1) to review the risk register and include risks and issues on the status reports. The risk management process is a step-by-step approach. Once a risk is identified, it is analyzed qualitatively (high, medium, or low), then treated (risk prevention and actions), followed by documenting the risk in the risk register. ITIL and project management standards (e.g., PMBOK® Guide and PRINCE2) have common purposes and are naturally aligned. Following the risk management process complies with international standards and dramatically improves the probability of project success. The risk management process appears in Figure 8.7, where the project team uses risk management throughout all the project phases.

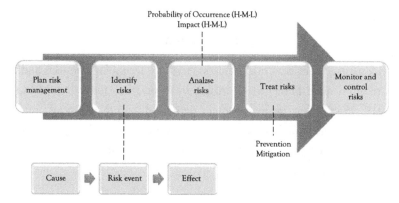

Figure 8.7 Risk management process

The project manager and team follow the risk management process and identify risks. Risk identification includes the risk cause, event, and effect (Table 8.3) and is documented following risk syntax. The important concept is the risk event is written with words that convey uncertainty that the risk may or may not occur; for example, we use words like *may*, *could*, and *might* to indicate the risk event has not yet occurred but could occur. When the proper risk syntax is used, understanding improves and communication risks are reduced. Thus, when we identify a risk, we frame the risk as a risk cause, event, and effect to aid effective and efficient analysis and treatment.

Table 8.3 Risk management framework and syntax

Element	Description	Syntax	Analysis	Treatment
Risk cause	Risks arise due to a cause or reason	*Due to* manufacturing delays	The probability the risk may occur: high, medium, or low probability of occurrence	Actions that can prevent this risk from occurring
Risk event	Something that may affect your project (positively or negatively)	*There is a risk* that the servers *may* arrive late	—	—
Risk effect	The consequence of the risk event occurring	*Resulting in* a delay in completing the build phase	If the risk occurs, the impact the risk event will have on the project: high, medium, or low impact	Actions that can mitigate (soften) the impact of the effect of the risk if the risk occurs

Once we identify and document the risk event (cause-event-effect), we can complete a qualitative risk analysis. First, we assess the probability of occurrence: the likelihood the risk cause may occur (Figure 8.7). Qualitative risk analysis assesses the probability of occurrence as high, medium, or low. There are quantitative techniques (e.g., Monte Carlo Simulation) that indicate that the probability of occurrence could be an 84.88 percent chance of occurring (high) or 24.116 percent chance of occurring (low). However, quantitative techniques are more cumbersome (e.g., risk modeling with statistical techniques), and the software can be expensive.

Additionally, many quantitative techniques take significant time to model and require large data sets. Instead, in *Shields Up*, qualitative techniques (high, medium, or low probability of occurrence) are used since they are easy to generate and understand. The project manager and contributing SME analyze the risk and agree upon the probability of occurrence.

Second, we analyze the effect the risk event will have on the project (e.g., a delay) if it occurs: we assess the impact (positive or negative) the effect will have on the project (high, medium, or low impact). Together the project manager and the SME analyze and agree upon the impact and then add their analysis to the risk register. The risk register is the primary tool the project team uses to manage risks and issues (Appendix 3); even though it is called a risk register, it is also used to manage issues (risks that have been realized and are project issues).

Once we identified the risk, understood the cause and effect, and analyzed the probability of occurrence and impact, we examine ways to treat the risk. First, we explore ways to prevent the risk from occurring. In our example about the server being delivered late due to manufacturing shortages, we can prevent the late delivery by ensuring the servers leave the factory on time, such as negotiating to pay a premium for the server or finding an alternative supplier. We can avoid the risk by purchasing a server model in stock and delivering it to meet our project schedule and not delay our build phase. Second, we look at mitigation actions to soften the impact if the risk occurs (e.g., we could not prevent the risk, and the risk becomes an issue). For example, we can complete other project activities to continue to progress. We might begin developing our test strategy, plan, and test scripts. At the same time, we wait for the servers to arrive (e.g., we may agree upon the contents and people responsible for their development). Again, we update the risk register of our mitigation actions; we delegate prevention and mitigation actions with a completion date. If we cannot prevent the risk by the risk resolution date, then the risk is converted into an issue.

Issues are risks that have been realized; the risk event cause was not prevented, the risk event occurred, and the project is affected. We analyze issues similarly to risks; however, the cause of the issue is the risk event. Since the issue has occurred, there is no probability of occurrence to consider: only the impact (high, medium, or low) and the issue's effect on the project. The issue syntax uses terms like *will* and *has* that convey 100 percent certainty the risk occurred and resulting in an issue (e.g., there is an issue that the servers *will* arrive late). We delegate the actions to resolve the issue and provide an issue resolution deadline. Thus, we have a risk register that supports how we manage risks and issues, who is responsible for preventing, mitigating, and resolving risks and issues.

Some projects benefit from a risk management workshop: key project stakeholders meet for about two hours to identify, analyze, and treat project risks and issues. First, describe your risk management plan for the project and give an overview of risk management theory. Use yellow stickies and instruct the participants to draw horizontal and vertical lines on the yellow stickies for the different elements of risk management (e.g., cause, event, effect probability, impact, prevention, and mitigation). Work together to identify the first few risks and show the participants how to complete the yellow stickies with risk information (Figure 8.8). Then ask the participants to identify some risks. This general approach allows participants to raise any risk and is designed to get the participants to work together and apply risk management theory. The participants place their risks onto the wall for everyone to see (collaborative software like online mind mapping tools can facilitate an online risk workshop). As participants write down risks, they actively contribute to the project and team building occurs.

We can then take a focused approach and systematically examine risks related to milestones, critical path, budget, phases, procurement process, go-live phase, and so on. For example, examine each activity along the critical path to identify, analyze, and treat risks and issues. We can repeat our risk management process to examine the main milestones, the schedule, the budget, and so on. By focusing on specific categories of risks, we are comprehensive and considerably shift the information curve.

Once risks are identified, we can then prioritize them with a risk matrix (Figure 8.9). We prioritize risks by their severity (probability × impact) and issues by impact (we do not assess probability of occurrence with issues since the issue exists). For example, high probability/high impact risks should be the team's focus as there is a high probability the risk may occur, and if it occurs, the impact on the project is high. We can

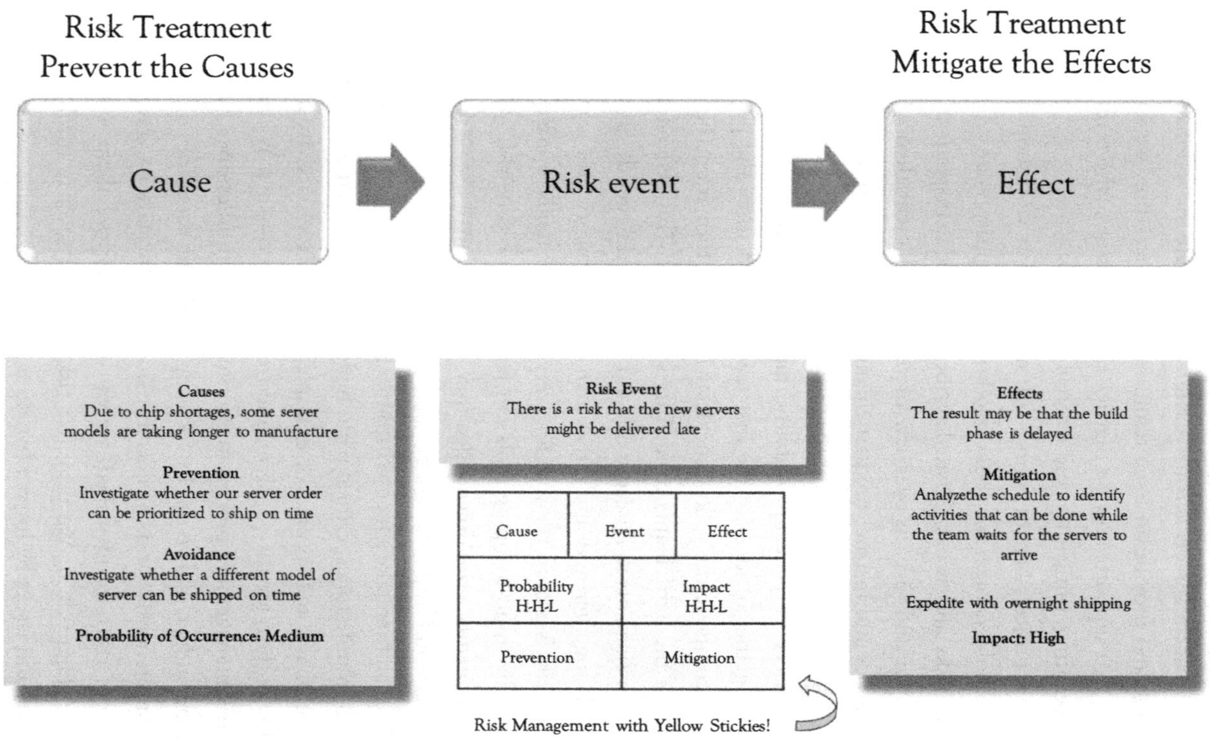

Risk Treatment
Prevent the Causes

Risk Treatment
Mitigate the Effects

Cause

Risk event

Effect

Causes
Due to chip shortages, some server models are taking longer to manufacture

Prevention
Investigate whether our server order can be prioritized to ship on time

Avoidance
Investigate whether a different model of server can be shipped on time

Probability of Occurrence: Medium

Risk Event
There is a risk that the new servers might be delivered late

Cause	Event	Effect
Probability H-H-L		Impact H-H-L
Prevention		Mitigation

Effects
The result may be that the build phase is delayed

Mitigation
Analyzethe schedule to identify activities that can be done while the team waits for the servers to arrive

Expedite with overnight shipping

Impact High

Risk Management with Yellow Stickies!

Figure 8.8 Risk identification, analysis, and treatment

then prioritize our risks, inform leadership of severe risks, and implement our treatment plans to prevent and mitigate. The risk register illustrates risk management efforts and becomes a historical record that should be preserved with other project documents (risk and issue registers can be used in disputes and litigation).

We also see in Figure 8.9 that we group natural triads on the yellow stickies: *cause–probability of occurrence–prevention* belong together, and *effect–impact–mitigation* belong together. Yellow stickies and the risk management workshop can be a powerful tool to quickly identify and understand risks and foster team building to shift the information curve for all.

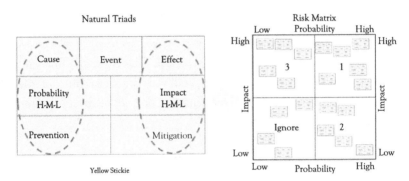

Figure 8.9 Risk matrix

Risk management is one of the most important activities we need to perform in our projects. Even though we have budgets and schedules, there is a high rate of technology projects delivered late or over budget. Why? Risks became issues resulting in delays and overspending. These project managers thought they had suitable budgets and schedules yet overspent and delivered late; the critical reason for their failure is that risk management was likely not as effective as necessary. Therefore, to significantly improve the probability of project success, we need to become effective and efficient with managing risks and issues, the core of hybrid project management used in our quest to deliver value.

Exercise

Think about your organization or another you worked for:

- How does your department manage and report risks and issues?
- Does your organization use Monte Carlo Simulation to help analyze risks?
- What is the IT project success rate in your industry?
- Review ISO 27005 Risk Management Process to deepen your understanding of information security risk management.

Microlearning

Investing in risk management skills is time well spent since all that we do in a cybersecurity ecosystem involves risk. Therefore, the following microlearning opportunities can expand your understanding of this important topic—project risk management. Look online for more information about:

- Risk management definition
- Risk, issue, and uncertainty definitions
- Risk management strategy
- Risk management plans
- Risk management templates
- Risk management tools
- Risk management matrix
- ISO 31000:2018 Risk Management—Guidelines
- Risk management and AI
- Monte Carlo Simulation and
- Risk management policy

Quality Management

Quality management includes tools and processes we use to ensure that the project will deliver the intended value for which it was initiated and documented in the quality management plan. We use training, templates, and checklists to help manage quality and other processes such as planning and tools like stage gates to verify the right quality is produced.

Shields Up uses two quality management processes: quality assurance and quality control (Figure 4.2). We do quality assurance before undertaking an activity to ensure the activity is performed correctly. We can follow a checklist, procedure, process, or template to improve the likelihood that the work will be completed to the right level of quality. Training also supplements quality assurance; for example, team members learn to use the risk register to document risks and issues consistently. Or we follow configuration instructions to set up a server. Quality control checks the work after it has been performed; we find and fix defects. Again, checklists, templates, procedures, and training can guide quality control activities to find and fix defects. For example, we follow testing scripts to verify that the build works as per the approved design. Thus, we use quality assurance and control to deliver the right amount of value in our projects: Quality *Assurance Before* Quality *Control: ABC.*

Our hybrid project management approach focuses on performing the work correctly the first time; we can improve the probability of project success (Done–Won–Who) with quality management and risk management. We favor quality assurance over quality control; it is better to perform the work resulting in minimal defects than finding and fixing defects as part of the quality control effort. Quality assurance with templates and checklists guides our work to be completed the first time correctly. Risk management (e.g., prevention activities) helps to ensure the work is done correctly.

We use governance techniques to help ensure high quality; for example, we structure our project with the traditional project management delivery approach with stage gates at the end of each phase to verify quality. If the team completes a high-quality design, the stakeholders approve the design, moving to the next phase. Risk and quality management are inherent in the hybrid project management approach, as seen in Figure 6.2. You can see that the risk management process occurs in each phase, and the stage gates act as a quality control mechanism. We follow templates (e.g., application detailed design) structured to keep our content lean and guide content development.

Thus far, we have met and planned in small groups with the sponsor and contributing SMEs. Our goal is to create a project plan to present to our project sponsor and leadership for approval to proceed with our project and leave the planning phase. We used the project charter/PID (project priority, scope, rationale, out of scope, WBS, Gantt chart, etc.) to orient and align our project team. We have a good understanding of our risks and issues and documented risks and issues in the risk register, and our project plan reflects a foundation of risk and issue management. Once we have a high-level plan, we schedule our first all-hands team meeting to "endorse" our project plan in a project planning workshop (PPW).

Project Planning Workshop

We exit the planning phase and begin the design phase when the project plan is approved (also known as the baselined project plan). The project plan contents vary according to the complexity and importance of the project, the audience who approves the project plan, and the reputation of the project manager. New project managers delivering complex and critical projects may need to develop more comprehensive plans.

The PPW brings together contributing stakeholders and the project sponsor. The high-level plan is presented for their endorsement before submitting it to leadership for formal approval (Figure 8.1).

1. **Background:** Begin by welcoming the PPW participants to the workshop and giving an overview of the workshop, to endorse the project plan. You can explain the delivery approach (e.g., predictive) and the governing stage gates.

2. **Scope:** Confirm the project scope, WBS, rationale, and out of scope items. The results of the three questions (Done–Won–Who) can be summarized, and the approved project priority using the Priority Triangle can also be presented. Ask if any key stakeholders have been missed. Some use an infographic project charter to align the stakeholders.

3. **Schedule:** Present the project schedule next. The goal is to get commitment from the stakeholders to contribute to the project according to the schedule. Show the high-level Gantt chart to orient the workshop attendees to the project timelines and see if it needs to be revised. Next, show the high-level network diagram that illustrates the schedule logic and critical path. The project manager discusses

key activities where broad involvement is required (e.g., design workshops, user acceptance testing, and training) and conveys that the project can be delayed if there is insufficient attendance. It is a perennial risk to get project participants to attend design workshops, training, and testing events when their operational tasks need to be completed, especially if that work is tracked to a service level agreement (e.g., incident resolution time). Therefore, it is beneficial to set expectations that the project can fail without their assistance. Again, we welcome stakeholder feedback.

4. **Budget:** The high-level project budget is presented for comments. However, the budget is sensitive in some projects and organizations and not presented in the PPW. (Your finance and procurement colleagues can assist you with procurement [e.g., vendor selection] if it has not already been completed.)

5. **People:** Project communications and resource management are presented. Effective communications will align with the project milestones, phases, and project priority. We communicate through meeting minutes and status reports. We use templates to guide content development (e.g., schedule and budgets) to share project information. The RACI chart can be used but might be too detailed for the PPW and may be reviewed separately.

6. **Risks and issues:** Finally, the main risks and issues are presented. The focus is on the prevention and mitigation actions necessary to deliver a successful project. The goal is to put preventative actions in place to reduce the probability of the risk occurring (e.g., reduce the probability from medium to low). We also want to reduce the impact of a risk if it occurs (e.g., reduce the severity from high to medium or even low). We describe how we use the risk register and its use in project meetings and status reports.

7. **Next steps:** We conclude the meeting with the next steps: the project manager updates the project plan with the PPW attendees' feedback and schedules a meeting with the project approvers to present the endorsed project plan with the project sponsor.

The PPW is an early milestone and brings together stakeholders to present an overview of the integrated project plan for their feedback. Presenting a project plan to others can be intimidating; however, practice and a systematic approach will position you well to succeed. There is a common risk in meetings and workshops that the discussion could be side-tracked and take the meeting in an unintended direction. One technique to keep the meeting on track is setting up a flipchart to "park" important items out of scope for the PPW (e.g., optimization after the project is terminated). With the PPW feedback incorporated into the plan, we use the project change control process to approve the updated project plan endorsed by the PPW participants. Since the PPW is an important milestone in each project, the many elements can become templates for future PPWs. Therefore, attention to design, layout, content flow, and messaging will pay future dividends when reused.

Project Change Management

We use the project change management process[2] (Figure 8.10) to approve the project plan and later to approve project changes (e.g., change the budget or schedule). Change management is fundamental to ITIL service management and is reflected in change enablement (Limited, AXELOS 2019, 112–115) and organizational change management practices (Limited, AXELOS 2019, 90–91). Managing project changes using a change management process is best practice.

The change management process begins with a request for a new project or a change to an existing project (e.g., change the schedule). The project manager analyzes the requested change (e.g., assesses feasibility and impact to the project and program) or develops a project plan. The project manager then presents the change or project plan to the decision makers. If the change or project plan is denied, the project manager informs the requester. If the change or project plan is approved, the project manager implements the change. Not seen in the change control diagram is the option for the approvers to require more information or

---

[2] Cross-functional flowcharts with "swim lanes" are an effective way to illustrate processes and task ownership. We use cross-functional flowcharts with Lean Six Sigma process optimization projects to document the as-is process and its "pain points." We optimize to re-draw the process to illustrate the reduction in steps and pain points. Drawing processes with cross-functional flowcharts is a useful skill for project participants.

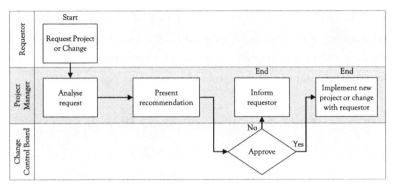

Figure 8.10 Change management process

request a change, and the project manager goes into an iterative cycle. These iterations can waste time; therefore, we want to avoid iterations and get approval the first time the change or project plan is presented.

While the project manager develops the project plan, he periodically updates the approvers, so their input also guides project plan development. Therefore, when the project plan is endorsed by the project contributors (e.g., SMEs), the approvers are already familiar with the project plan. Before the change control meeting where the approvers will approve or reject the project plan, the project manager informally previews the high-level plan with the committee approvers and revises where necessary. The result is the approvers will be ready to approve the project plan in the change control meeting and you will avoid revision iterations. Previewing proposed changes with the approvers works the same way: get endorsement before the meeting to increase the probability the approvers will approve your project plan in the change control meeting.

To improve the probability of success with the change control process, try to understand your audience's expectations; what do the approvers want? We can tell the story the project plan was developed collaboratively with the stakeholders and endorsed. The approvers are interested in key risks and issues and your treatment plans. They also want to know how you will keep them informed throughout the project. Therefore, you can increase the likelihood of approval through collaboration, develop your project plan on a risk management foundation, and follow a hybrid project management approach. Some organizations follow an "approval chain," beginning with business/sponsor approvals and ending with senior IT leadership approvals. The rationale is to have the business representatives approve the project plan first; once they approve, IT will approve. After the project plan is approved, archive the meeting's minutes that provide your approval to proceed.

Ubiquitous Cybersecurity Planning

It is good practice to build cybersecurity into our projects rather than adding cybersecurity as the project prepares to go live. There are many resources to guide project planning to include cybersecurity, including the ISO 27002 Information Technology-Security Techniques-Code of Practice for Information Security Controls (ISO 2018a, 1–90):

1. Ensure the development and test environments are secure.
2. Add security requirements to the design.
3. Include security within the milestones.

Systematic project planning can shift the information curve and improve the probability of cybersecurity project success.

Plan Phase: Final Thoughts

Project planning is a fundamental part of the project and critical to success. When one assesses the root cause of project failure, insufficient planning and risk management are often cited along with inadequate testing. Therefore, allow sufficient time to plan your project. Following an integrated and lean planning process can increase the probability of project success. We aim to learn more about the project sooner to avoid costly changes later in the project. We can shift the information curve with project planning tools like the Project Management Gizmo, Priority Triangle, Done–Won–Who, and PLOs. These tools reveal essential information like risks and issues; following the risk management process brings risks and issues under control.

We apply quality assurance and control techniques like reusing templates to reduce risks. We plan and design in security so that the technology we deliver is more likely to fit within our technology ecosystem.

One message we need to give is that our project can fail. However, we are more likely to succeed with stakeholder, sponsor, and leadership engagement. Finally, we package the project plan as a professional report with branding, attractive layout, and design. A comprehensive and appealing design gives the reader confidence that they have chosen the right project manager.

Microlearning

Project planning is a skill that improves with use. The following topics can improve your understanding and application of project management and improve the probability of project success. Search online for the following topics to deepen your understanding of project planning:

- How to make a project communications plan?
- How to use a risk register?
- Search for "project planning templates."
- Search for "project planning software."

CHAPTER 9

Design Phase

Projects are initiated to deliver a product or service. The design phase is to develop a design for the product or service based on user requirements. Technology projects often have multiple design documents, such as the application detailed design, low-level infrastructure design, and integration design. The goal is to document the design collaboratively developed with the product or service users and then approve the design. Thus, end users and the technical team work together to develop a design that is submitted for approval. Some organizations have business analysts to assist with design activities and requirements elicitation and documentation. Once the design is approved, the project team moves to the next phase, where the technical team works to build the product or service according to the approved design. Systems analysis and design is a core topic in information systems programs at the postsecondary level and outside our project management perspective scope. However, project managers oversee the design phase and should be familiar with systems analysis and design basics.

Design Phase Best Practices

The ITIL 4 provides detailed guidance on designing a service and guides the reader to take a holistic design approach. Quality, risk, and project management contribute to a design that delights the end user. However, full value is unlikely to be delivered if such a holistic approach is not followed (Limited, AXELOS 2019, 34). The design can also be improved by using design thinking techniques (Defossez, McMillan, and Vuppala 2020, 4) and the Lean Six Sigma approach to optimize a process. For example, we can improve our design by designing-in cybersecurity functionality rather than addressing cybersecurity as an afterthought during the transition to the production environment phase.

The project team needs to consider the risks throughout the project and are guided by ITIL's risk management practice (Limited, AXELOS 2019, 95–97). An example of applying risk management to design is to apply the Cybersecurity Golden Rule: don't build what you cannot adequately protect (Skilton and Hovsepian 2018, 207). We are also reminded that we can fail without a thorough project plan and not following good design practices (Limited, AXELOS 2019, 132–134). If you get the design right and follow a lean approach to implement the design, you are more likely to optimize value.

A common approach to documenting the project requirements and design is to meet with the end users in a series of design workshops. The basic process is to meet in a workshop setting to elicit the design from stakeholders, document the required design in a design document(s), and then approve the design. Once approved, the design phase ends, and the build phase begins. A common risk is that the workshops might not be fully attended, resulting in a flawed or incomplete design being approved and then built. During testing, the users will inform the technical team that the design is "defective." Therefore, one needs to prevent and mitigate poor workshop attendance. One prevention measure is to invite managers to the workshop. Their attendance conveys the workshop's importance. If one's boss attends, the worker is more likely to attend the workshop. One mitigation action is to repeat workshops for critical SMEs who may miss a design workshop. While repeating workshops can be resource intensive, adding additional workshops to accommodate principal SME's input is sometimes unavoidable to progress according to the schedule.

The project manager may use a design template from the PMO to document the design. Templates are a quality assurance aid and are used to develop a design document expediently. (You can find ITIL compliant design templates and workshop agendas online if your organization does not have its own.) The design document(s) needs to be approved as with the project plan. We can take a similar approval approach as we did in the planning phase. We inform the approvers of our progress, listen, incorporate their feedback, and then circulate the design document to the approvers for their approval. Once the design document is approved, the design phase ends. The technical team begins the build phase by building the product or service according to the specification in the design document(s).

Design Phase: Final Thoughts

The design phase produces a design that can be built and tested that meets the end-user's expectations. Value is designed with the end users in design workshops. Business analysts specialize in elaborating and documenting the design, requirements, reports, and other elements. Our goal is to produce a design that accurately reflects the end-user's and sponsors' expectations from a project management perspective. The project manager schedules a series of design workshops and invites different team members to complete designs like a detailed application design, an integration design, and a low-level infrastructure design. There is a potentially high impact risk that not all required SMEs may attend the scheduled workshop due to other priorities. Therefore, one may mitigate representation gaps by scheduling additional workshops. Once the design is documented, it is circulated to the SMEs for their feedback. The feedback is used to update the design documents and is circulated for approval.

Microlearning

Critical work is completed in the design phase, and there have been many advances related to improving design. Prior to searching online, review the microlearning activities in the "Technology Analysis" section in Chapter 7 as they may relate to design phase activities. Search online for:

- What are the steps in systems analysis and design?
- How does ITIL work?
- How does ITIL 3 service design work?
- What is service catalog management? Capacity management? Availability management? Service continuity management? and so on
- How does the ITIL 4 business analysis practice work?

- What is design thinking?
- What is business process design?
- What is a design workshop agenda?
- How do we document a design?
- "ITIL service design templates"

CHAPTER 10

Build Phase

The focus of the build phase is to follow the requirements in the design document(s) and build the product or service. Building is a technical effort, and it often requires minimal overview from the project manager other than to track and control progress according to the schedule. The ITIL Service Value System guides the build phase, where the project team works together as a system to build the service for the user (Limited, AXELOS 2019, 17–18). Some organizations document the build in an "as-built" document. Once the product or service has been built, and the build stage gate criteria are satisfied, the project moves to the test phase.

Microlearning

Following are some exercises to enhance your understanding of the build phase:

- How does as-built documentation work?
- What are the best practices for as-built documentation?
- Search for "build phase templates."

CHAPTER 11

Test Phase

Now that the product or service is built, we move to the test phase and plan testing (Figure 6.2). Testing is a quality control activity: find and fix defects. We are fortunate to have consistent and broad guidance from quality, service, and project management specialties to apply to testing activities. (The NIST cybersecurity framework is operationally focused, and testing during a cybersecurity project is not directly addressed.) For example, the ISO 9001:2000 quality management standard guides the user on how to deliver products and services: "In planning product realization, the organization shall determine the following, as appropriate: … c) required verification, validation, monitoring, inspection, and test activities specific to the product and the criteria for product acceptance; …" (ISO 2000, 30). We are guided to test and involve our stakeholders to verify the value we are delivering. Testing is critical to quality management and is considered a critical success factor in *Shields Up*.

Testing during a project is directly addressed in ITIL's Service Value System in its General Management Practices—Testing (Limited, AXELOS 2019, 24). *Shields Up* is aligned with the ITIL approach to delivering capability and includes the build, test, and deliver (T2P) phases (Figure 6.2, the project delivery approach—project phases). However, you can begin developing the test strategy and plan earlier in the project if you have spare capacity. Again, you can use templates or a previous test strategy and plan as a starting point.

Testing is an integral part of project management; for example, testing is part of the PMBOK® Guides. "During the planning phase, the project manager and team determine how to test or inspect the product, deliverable, or service to meet the stakeholders' needs and expectations…" (PMI 2017a, 285). The PMI standard frames testing as a phase within the project life cycle: "Test. Final quality review and inspection of deliverables are carried out before transition, go-live or acceptance by the customer" (PMI 2021, 105). Thus, testing is a critical quality control activity embedded in quality management, service management, and project management standards and a central component in the *Shields Up* hybrid project management approach. We can begin developing a test strategy and plan as early as the planning phase on some projects and continue its development through to the test phase.

Test Strategy

Begin test planning by developing a test strategy and test plan. The test strategy may include a diagram of the testing process (Figure 11.1) to illustrate the process and participants.

The testing process diagram (Figure 11.1) does not illustrate the collaborative nature of planning the test strategy and plan; the project manager sets expectations for testing involvement when he meets with the sponsor and leadership early in the project and during the project planning workshop. Some organizations include a test strategy and plan approval process with a stage gate before testing commencement.

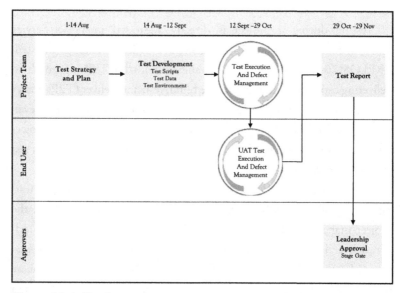

Figure 11.1 Testing process

A test strategy is a concise report to stakeholders that outlines at a macro-level the testing approach and how the test objectives will be satisfied. The following are the basics of a test strategy and can be tailored to your project:

1. **Test objectives**: Document and verify the test objectives (e.g., find and fix defects, improve confidence in the product or service, and verify the product or service meets expectations).
2. **In scope**: Identify what will be tested and why.
3. **Out of scope**: Document what will be excluded from testing and why.
4. **Test type**: Identify and justify the types of tests you will use (Table 11.1). Some add a "Rationale" column to justify why a particular test is in scope or out of scope. A search online reveals additional tests (e.g., smoke testing), and the reader can review this technical theory and practice to tailor the types of tests appropriate for the project.

Table 11.1 System testing overview

Test type	Included	Due date	Responsible
Unit	Yes	12 September	Jason Hawk
Functional	Yes	17 September	Saif Al Llama
Integration	Yes	24 September	Makoto Tamari
Regression	No	—	—
Install/uninstall	Yes	1 October	Federico Sant Anna
Performance/stress	Yes	1 October	Irene Cornell
User acceptance	Yes	15 October	Marianne Jones
Security	Yes	29 October	Israa Alberta

5. **Test execution**: Describe and justify whether testing will be manual or automated. Some tests may be automated (e.g., functional), while others may be manual (e.g., unit). There is an increasing number of open source and commercial testing tools, and many incorporate defect management.
6. **Defect management**: Describe how defects will be managed and controlled and the software that you will use to manage the defects,

including any outstanding actions (e.g., defects that are resolved with future software patches from the vendor).

7. **Communications management**: Describe how stakeholders will be informed of test results, including the final test report.

8. **Test schedule**: Include a high-level schedule or Gantt chart.

9. **Test risk and issue management**: Describe that you will use the defect management process in conjunction with the risk management process. If significant defects are identified, a risk or an issue may be raised and managed.

Some organizations have a test strategy and plan template (quality assurance) to guide the project manager. The project manager can front-end load the project by collecting test strategy and other project-related templates early in the project to help guide project planning.

Test Plan

The test plan is an extension of and companion to the test strategy. The test plan provides the details of the test environment, test scripts, and test data. The subject matter experts (e.g., vendor) usually take the lead to develop the test plan:

1. **Test environment**: The test environment mirrors the production environment and is safe for testing and experimental defect resolution. The test environment includes the hardware, software, and operating system that meets the minimum requirements for test execution.

2. **Test scripts**: Develop the detailed test instructions to test and verify that the requirements have been met (e.g., Load the website landing page and click on the "Login" button. Verify that the Login Screen appears with the Username and Password fields). Some distinguish test scripts (automated testing) from test cases (manual testing). Test scripts often include the test ID number, test data, testing steps, and actual and expected results. If the actual results differ from the expected results, there may be a defect.

3. **Test data**: Data used during the test is developed rather than using real data due to privacy concerns. The project team develops data to use in the test scripts to verify that the system operates as designed. Since the data are developed, a lean-oriented team can develop versatile data to service multiple test scripts. Many testers leverage data management tools to reduce the administrative burden of test data management.

4. **Test metrics**: Identify the metrics that the approvers desire (e.g., number of test scripts planned, number of test scripts executed, and number of defects); sometimes, testers provide metrics that are not required from approvers. Set up your testing dashboard to track the required metrics and easily add them to the test report.

The reader is fortunate that an online search can refresh their knowledge of test environments, test scripts, data, and metrics and show the current state and trends in application testing (e.g., automated testing with AI capabilities).

The test plan may include a requirements traceability matrix that maps the stakeholders' requirements to test scripts and tracks verification (Figure 11.2). The matrix is used as evidence that the project requirements have been met. The requirements traceability matrix is a quality assurance

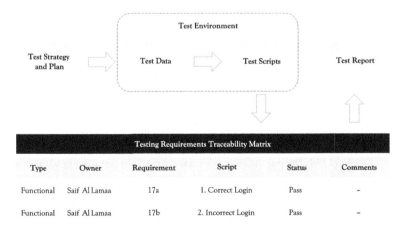

Testing Requirements Traceability Matrix					
Type	Owner	Requirement	Script	Status	Comments
Functional	Saif Al Lamaa	17a	1. Correct Login	Pass	–
Functional	Saif Al Lamaa	17b	2. Incorrect Login	Pass	–

Figure 11.2 Requirements traceability matrix

template that can be reused in future projects. The requirements traceability matrix can serve as a testing dashboard by adding status and results columns. Adding additional columns is an example of leanness in project documents. Testing applications increasingly offer cohesive support for managing the test environment, data, scripts, and defects management, while some testers use spreadsheets to guide and track testing. When testing is complete, the requirements traceability matrix can be included in the appendixes of the final test report.

User Acceptance Testing

User acceptance tests (UAT) verify if a system satisfies the approved stakeholder requirements. The UAT occurs after the testing team completes their series of tests (e.g., unit, functional, and integration), rectifies defects, and the SMEs believe the system performs as designed. Then, the project manager invites the end users to UAT testing workshops (Figure 11.1) to validate that the system performs as designed and meets stakeholder expectations. The testing team repeats the tests and uses the requirements traceability dashboard, test environment, scripts, and data. Ideally, the end user executes the scripts to understand the system better, resulting in finding and fixing defects before going live. The term "defects" is broadly used to mean the end user requires changes. For example, the system may operate as designed. Still, the user may request changes to menus—rather than a menu list in alphabetical order; the user may request the top five choices be prioritized and appear at the top of the drop-down menu. Or there could be spelling and grammar mistakes to fix. These defects are fixed and tracked to completion with the requirements traceability matrix or a testing dashboard. If there are any outstanding defects or comments, they are also noted in the traceability matrix and defects tracker.

During UAT, the end user sees the system perform for the first time and may request design changes, even though the design has been approved. Should the end user request significant changes that may challenge the completion schedule or otherwise, the project manager may raise a risk that testing may be late. Sometimes the requested design changes can be deferred to a postproject optimization phase and not delay your project.

Requests for significant changes are often traced back to the design phase and the quality of the end user involvement. Therefore, the project manager is prudent to ensure that end users are fully engaged in design workshops and design document review. Should the end user not be fully engaged in the design phase, then the project manager may raise a risk during the design phase that the test phase may take longer to complete due to requests for changes to the approved design.

To complete the design phase, some project managers review the design document with the approving end user during a two-hour meeting and reduce the risk of not understanding the design. In *Shields Up,* we focus on preventing risks rather than resolving issues (e.g., quality assurance efforts are emphasized). Once the end users complete UAT testing and give their approval, the requirements traceability matrix is updated, and the approvals are recorded in meeting minutes or in an e-mail. The project manager then completes the test report; the last stage gate to leave the test phase.

Test Report

The test report contains the testing results and is prepared by the project manager (Table 11.2). The purpose of the test report is to document test results as outlined in the test strategy and test plan to determine whether sufficient quality exists and if the product or service is ready for release. It is prudent to refer to the test strategy and plan when writing the test report to ensure completeness.

A search online will bring many examples of test reports and templates that can guide the project manager and team to tailor their test report to their project and audience. The test report is developed and sent to the project stakeholders for approval. Once approved, the test phase is completed, and the transition to production phase begins.

Finally, before proceeding to the transition to production phase (T2P), some cybersecurity projects do not lend themselves to technical testing such as an audit or training project; however, there is still a role for quality assurance and quality control. For example, one can use peer reviews to find defects in a cybersecurity audit; a colleague can review the audit results to find any defects. After a cybersecurity training course is

Table 11.2 Test report contents

	Contents	Comments
Main body	Test report overview	State the purpose of testing and overall results (e.g., the testing was successful), the first content the reader looks for in a test report. You may add the UAT was successful, the end users verified the system's quality, and is ready for release
	Test results	List the testing metrics and highlight key points or anomalies of interest
	Defects	List defects encountered and resolved and any outstanding defects. Refer the reader to the Appendix—Outstanding Actions—for the defect resolution plan
	Conclusion	Restate the overall results and emphasize that testing is complete
Appendixes	Application overview	Provide a brief overview of the software application should the reader be unfamiliar with its functionality. Identify integration points, cloud storage, security, etc.
	Test environment, data, and tools overview	Provide an overview and assessment of the test environment, data, and tools used to test the application
	Testing scope	Identify in-scope and out-of-scope testing. Address any testing that was not executed and the rationale. The complete requirements traceability matrix may show the testing scope and the types of tests performed
	Outstanding actions	List any outstanding actions required to complete testing or fix defects. Some raise a service ticket for each action with a future completion date to coincide with resource availability or patch release to fix a defect
	Lessons learned	Identify lessons learned regarding test environment, test data, tools, testing process, etc.

developed, it is best practice to pilot test the training to determine if the learning outcomes are met (e.g., complete a quality control check).

Test Phase: Final Thoughts

Along with planning, the testing phase is critical to project success. As the criticality and importance of the project increases, so does testing comprehensiveness and formality. Testing is a quality control exercise; if the requirements definition was correctly executed (quality assurance), then there should be few defects in the testing phase. The test plan and strategy guide testing, and the test report documents results and next steps. These documents can form a set of templates for future testing. We first test the system to find and fix defects, and then we invite the end users to participate in UAT. They verify that the requirements have been met and that the service is ready for operations. If there is any incomplete testing or outstanding actions, we note them and perhaps raise tickets for future action.

Microlearning

Testing technology has seen advances in testing the process and technologies. Search online and discover:

- How does ITIL service validation and testing work?
- How does technology defect management work?
- How do you track testing defects?
- What is the best testing software?
- How does automated testing work?
- Download test strategy, test plan, and test report templates for future use.

CHAPTER 12

Transition to Production

The transition to production (T2P) phase includes those activities to hand over the product or service produced through the project delivery approach to the operations team. ITIL's Release Management (Limited, AXELOS 2019, 125–127) guides a broad range of activities such as:

1. Delivering the service with a waterfall or agile delivery method.
2. Ensuring that the new release can be tracked, verified, uninstalled, and backed out of the production environment if necessary.
3. Certifying deviations, risks, and issues can be managed and controlled.
4. Completing knowledge and skills transfer to operations.

Add cybersecurity activities to this list to bring the service or product into the production environment, such as adding the new product or service to the Security Information and Event Management (SIEM) system, conducting penetration testing, and revoking the vendor's passwords.

Transition to production planning can begin in the planning phase and is finished in the T2P phase. For example, cybersecurity should be designed into the product or service to meet cybersecurity requirements and have a smooth going-live path (ISO 2018a, 7). Critical to ITIL release and deployment, management success is the seamless transition between projects and operations for new services (Limited, AXELOS 2019, 143–145). Therefore, we develop formal plans to safely release the service to our end users to improve the probability of success and align with "do-it-once" thinking.

The ITIL release management processes and tools guide project participants to develop and improve the capabilities to transition new and changed IT services into operations (Limited, AXELOS 2019, 125–127).

Successful project managers create and reuse T2P checklists to guide the final project actions to take the product or service live.

T2P Checklist

Transition to production checklists act like a quality assurance guide to ensure that the tail end of the project is "tight, rather than loose." That is, the final go-live activities to transition from a project phase to operations are planned, managed, and controlled to improve the probability of a successful implementation and adoption. T2P checklists vary by project and organization; however, common tasks must be completed to smooth service transition. Involve the deployment manager early in the project to plan your release and deployment actions and to create a lean T2P checklist:

1. Inform the change authorization board (CAB) that a new service is preparing to go live. Astute project managers add an agenda item to the CAB meeting as much as two to three months or more prior to going live to raise the visibility of their project. They also inform the CAB that they use a T2P checklist to manage and control go-live activities to improve confidence in a methodical release.
2. Test the backup/restore capabilities.
3. Remove vendor access as appropriate.
4. Add the new service to the information systems management system.
5. Develop and add an FAQ for the new service to the service operations manual.
6. Train the support desk.
7. Train the end users.
8. Perform a vulnerability assessment and remediation.
9. Complete a system hardening review.
10. Conduct an information system risk review.
11. Complete a disaster recovery test.
12. Develop a go-live communications plan including prepared communications to address risks (e.g., an unsuccessful implementation requiring an uninstall from the production environment).
13. Set up a go-live command center for critical and priority projects.
14. And so on.

In line with best practices, the project manager completes only the T2P actions required to release the service to the end users. The services are valued and optimized; tailoring is applied to project planning and service transition activities.

One of the final T2P actions is getting CAB's approval to release the new service into the production environment. (Some projects do not involve systems released into the production environment like cybersecurity audits but may require a report or presentation.) Using the change management process is essential since system misconfigurations are a prominent attack vector and can be better managed with a systematic and formal review before being released into the production environment (Microsoft 2020, 74). The project manager coordinates the release date with the project schedule and a CAB meeting. Some projects benefit from the project manager discussing the release with CAB approving members before the meeting to provide detailed answers to any questions.

When your release is ready to be discussed during the CAB meeting, begin by explaining the T2P process you followed (e.g., checklist and raising tickets for T2P services) to win confidence that your service is ready to be released and that the stakeholders endorse the release. Your message is "good process, good result." For more critical and impactful projects, consider using an infographic or a dashboard (Table 12.1) to explain that the release is ready to be deployed, the organization is ready for the release, and you have a plan to monitor and control the release. You strive to make approval easy by providing information CAB approvers desire.

Once permission to proceed is provided by the CAB, it is time to follow your go-live plan. Some projects benefit from practicing their go-live, including restore backout, and escalation procedures. Quality is improved with checklists to guide go-live activities supported with short "standup" meetings. These T2P procedures contribute to a smooth and predictable go live.

T2P: Final Thoughts

Our goal is to seamlessly transfer the product or service produced by the project into operations with the intended outcomes. We complete the T2P actions identified as early as the planning phase to release the service into the production environment, including backout plans. We include

Table 12.1 CAB go-live status report

Release elements	Status	Comments
Cybersecurity readiness	Green	List the security actions that have been completed and the state of readiness
Systems readiness	Green	Ready
New service readiness	Green	Ready
Operational readiness	Green	Some training is outstanding; however, the sponsor confirms the organization is ready
Training status	Amber	11% of the organization has not completed training; additional training is being provided. 95% of the organization will be trained by Week 2 (post go-live)
Communications readiness	Green	Ready—including backout communications
Reporting readiness	Green	Ready—escalation procedures distributed
Support readiness	Green	Ready—simulation exercises complete
Risks	Green	No high severity risks; under control
Issues	Green	No high severity issues; under control
Other	—	None

training and communications to ensure a seamless transition. We work with the CAB and the release manager to plan and release the service into the production environment.

Microlearning

Following are some practical exercises to enhance your learning. Search online for:

- ITIL release management
- ITIL release management templates
- ITIL release management practice
- Release strategies (e.g., canary/dark release)
- Change authorization board

CHAPTER 13

Monitor, Stabilize, and Close Out

The service or product has been delivered to operations, and the project team transitions to support (early life support) and closeout activities. ITIL's Service Value Chain's last activities are to deliver and support the new service according to users' expectations and specifications. The team looks for feedback about the quality of the release and stays close to the end users. The project team receives service success feedback to guide support and future optimization planning. Some projects benefit from a go-live command center that gathers the project and operational resources for immediate ticket resolution and reporting escalation. The go-live plan will have predetermined trigger points to escalate and report issues and trigger points to uninstall and back the new service out of the production environment.

One way to monitor the quality of the new service is to monitor incidents. ITIL provides guidelines in its Incident Management practice. The project manager will likely review daily incident reports, if any, to understand adoption and quality. For example, key performance indicators (KPIs) are monitored (e.g., resolution times) and compared to service level agreements (SLAs). When examining the incidents, categorize the incidents into technical and training-related incidents to better understand the quality of the implementation. Project managers often establish closeout stage gates based on tickets/day or tickets/week or close out the project a predetermined monitoring period (e.g., four weeks). While the project team monitors and supports the new service, they work concurrently on closeout activities like auditing contracts for compliance. Once the closeout metric has been reached, the project is closed out.

The purpose of the closeout process is to formally terminate the project, transfer the product or service to the sponsor, and release project resources. Some project managers use a checklist to guide closeout activities such as:

1. **Deliverable handover:** Formally transfer the deliverables to the sponsor and verify acceptance in meeting minutes or an e-mail. The requirements traceability matrix can be used (Figure 11.2), and columns include links to confirming meeting minutes or e-mails.
2. **Project completion notice:** Inform all stakeholders that the requirements have been delivered and the project is completed. Direct the stakeholders to contact the service desk if they need assistance.
3. **Contract closeout:** Review the contracts to ensure that all contractual obligations have been met. Some project managers use the requirements traceability matrix to document whether contract obligations have been met.
4. **Resources:** Release resources (people and equipment) and celebrate with your team.
5. **Lessons learned:** Complete a lessons learned exercise with the project stakeholders considering what went well and what can be improved.

Document these actions in a closeout report and archive project documents for future reference. Inform the sponsor by e-mail that the project is closed out (terminated) and add the notification to the project archives.

Lessons learned is a common practice in many organizations. What went well? What did we struggle with? What should we stop doing? What should we continue to do? And other questions help to learn, which is a cornerstone in all frameworks that guide good practice and hybrid project management in *Shields Up*. Closeout reports often include a lessons learned section. However, the lessons are often collected but not always learned; why do we have dismal and recurring project failure rates? Therefore, my recommendation is to complete lessons learned at the beginning of the project and the start of each project phase. During team meetings, these can be short discussions to apply the wisdom and knowledge developed on previous projects. Not only can we apply previous learnings, but the team values having their input implemented. Lessons learned can be implemented more effectively when the lessons are prioritized and assigned to a person to complete with a tracked and reported deadline.

Microlearning

Search online for more information about the tail end of projects; a strong finish is the preferred way to terminate projects:

- How to terminate a project?
- How to complete a lessons learned exercise?
- Locate contract closeout templates and contract closeout letters?
- Find project closeout best practices?

CHAPTER 14

Operations and Optimize

When the project is closed out, operations manage the service delivered through your project. ITIL provides a framework, tools, and processes to manage and optimize the service. Remnants of the project may remain; there may be tickets on hold to complete outstanding project actions. For example, a requirement might not have been satisfied due to a defect fixed with a future patch. Vendors have their release strategy and schedule for patches and upgrades. The outstanding ticket can remind operations to look for the patch and plan its release to satisfy outstanding functionality.

The Lean Six Sigma approach to optimization coupled with ITIL's and ISO 9001's continual improvement provides frameworks and tools to optimize products and services to deliver more value. Optimization will be more successful if proven processes are followed, like the Lean Six Sigma DMAIC problem solving and optimization process. Optimization proposals can result in new projects and initiatives along the Service Value Chain.

Some projects take an iterative and phased approach (endorsed by ITIL), beginning with a minimum install. Once the basics are installed ("vanilla install") and used, end users better understand what should be optimized and extended. Optimization can trigger new projects that can be considered using the change control process to provide approval to proceed with the new project.

CHAPTER 15

Conclusion

When we read about digital transformation, we see evidence we are entering a period of colossal digital-driven change such as quantum computing and AI leveraged research in health care (IBM 2021, 1–2). The way we live and work is quickly changing due to an increased pace of technology adoption. Businesses are forging strategies enabled with technology and innovation. One implication of this uptake in technology is the demand and priority for cybersecurity services have increased. The threat landscape and associated vulnerabilities have greatly expanded. Businesses are increasing their technology and cybersecurity budgets but require the CISO to justify and demonstrable a return on investment.

With increased cybersecurity work and larger budgets, organizations actively recruit cybersecurity professions ranging from entry-level roles to specialized roles like cloud security specialists and cybersecurity project managers. Unfortunately, the demand for cybersecurity talent far exceeds the supply. The cybersecurity skill gap creates problems for businesses, such as delaying cybersecurity projects until a cybersecurity project manager is available to complete the project. The skill gap also creates opportunities for cybersecurity professionals to lead their first project. With leadership comes the responsibility for outcomes: project success. Therefore, project managers are more likely to deliver successful projects following a structured rather than an ad hoc project management delivery approach.

Organizations increasingly rely on technology to deliver products and services and keep our information confidential, private, and secure. Organizations adapt best practices and frameworks to provide a structured approach to delivering products and services that meet approved requirements and service level agreements. Organizations rarely apply the standards and frameworks as designed; instead, they pick and choose the elements required to meet their requirements (e.g., they tailor the

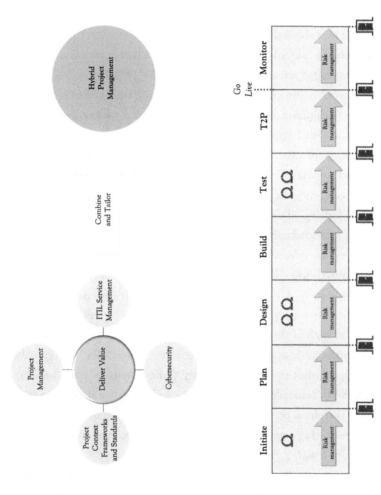

Figure 15.1 Shields Up hybrid project management

framework to their specific situation). We see tailoring guidance in project management standards like the PMBOK® Guide and ITIL to pick the essential project management tools and processes required to deliver a successful project (Figure 15.1). The focus of hybrid project management documented in *Shields Up* is to follow a structured approach to meet stakeholder needs and leverage opportunities to deliver value to the end users. The traditional project management delivery approach is appropriate for most projects. It has a foundation of risk management to improve the probability that value will be delivered to the service users. We may include iterative work to determine the best design or fix a defect found during testing. However, most cybersecurity projects can be implemented with the traditional project management delivery approach with iterations when required. While our project management approach may vary from project to project, our hybrid project management principles do not; we have a sense of urgency, encourage collaboration, and focus on delivering value.

Congratulations for making it thus far! You may want to review specific chapters, review the exercises, and complete the microlearning actions. Project management is a dynamic specialty attracting new practitioners and researchers each year, resulting in best practice maturity and new ways of work. Couple the advances in technology and cybersecurity with project management, we have a dynamic environment to plan, implement, and sustain value. Our journey to learn about project management continues.

PART III

Appendixes

APPENDIX 1

NIST Cybersecurity Framework Core Example

The National Institute of Standards and Technology (NIST) Framework for Improving Critical Infrastructure Cybersecurity is a leading global cybersecurity framework. Therefore, all IT professionals, including cybersecurity professionals, should be aware of the NIST Framework since everyone has a role in cybersecurity. The NIST standard is arranged according to functions, categories, subcategories, and references (Table A1.1; National Institute of Standards and Technology 2018, 50).

The NIST Framework helps organizations audit their cybersecurity capabilities, identify gaps, and set targets for improvements (more projects). Leading a cybersecurity audit or broader technology audit are good development projects as they are nontechnical and provide an overview of systems and services.

Table A1.1 NIST cybersecurity framework core example

Function	Category	Subcategory	References
Recover	**Recovery Planning (RC.RP):** Recovery processes and procedures are executed and maintained to ensure restoration of systems or assets affected by cybersecurity incidents	**RC.RP-1:** Recovery plan is executed during or after a cybersecurity incident	**CIS CSC 10** **COBIT 5** APO12.06, DSS02.05, DSS03.04 **ISO/IEC 27001:2013** A.16.1.5 **NIST SP 800-53 Rev. 4** CP-10, IR-4, IR-8
	Improvements (RC. IM): Recovery planning and processes are improved by incorporating lessons learned into future activities	**RC.IM-1:** Recovery plans incorporate lessons learned	**COBIT 5** APO12.06, BAI05.07, DSS04.08 **ISA 62443-2-1:2009** 4.4.3.4 **ISO/IEC 27001:2013** A.16.1.6, Clause 10 **NIST SP 800-53 Rev. 4** CP-2, IR-4, IR-8
		RC.IM-2: Recovery strategies are updated	**COBIT 5** APO12.06, BAI07.08 **ISO/IEC 27001:2013** A.16.1.6, Clause 10 **NIST SP 800-53 Rev. 4** CP-2, IR-4, IR-8
	Communications (RC.CO): Restoration activities are coordinated with internal and external parties (e.g., coordinating centers, Internet Service Providers, owners of attacking systems, victims, other CSIRTs, and vendors)	**RC.CO-1:** Public relations are managed	**COBIT 5** EDM03.02 **ISO/IEC 27001:2013** A.6.1.4, Clause 7.4
		RC.CO-2: Reputation is repaired after an incident	**COBIT 5** MEA03.02 **ISO/IEC 27001:2013** Clause 7.4
		RC.CO-3: Recovery activities are communicated to internal and external stakeholders as well as executive and management teams	**COBIT 5** APO12.06 **ISO/IEC 27001:2013** Clause 7.4 **NIST SP 800-53 Rev. 4** CP-2, IR-4

APPENDIX 2

Project Management Gizmo

The Project Management Gizmo[1] is a research-based tool to assess a project to understand the project's complexity (Table A2.1) and the effort required (Table A2.2) to deliver the project successfully (Skulmoski 2008, 1). One can use the Gizmo to systematically assess a project to improve their front-end understanding to develop better project plans.

The Gizmo becomes even more valuable when project stakeholders independently assess the project and compare their results. When used in a group setting, the Gizmo will help identify areas of alignment and misalignment. For example, the project manager might assess the type of work and give the effort to implement the technology a low score. In contrast, the implementing consultants give the effort to implement a higher score. The two then discuss why the scores are different and come to a consensus. Without the Gizmo, the project manager might underestimate the effort to implement the technology resulting in a schedule with insufficient time.

Using the Gizmo improves the teams' understanding of the project and aligns the team, resulting in better project plans. The Gizmo guides the team to analyze the project systematically and helps the team shift the information curve. For example, the team may identify risks related to effort complexity or competency gaps revealed with the Gizmo. Once identified with the Gizmo, risks can be managed with the risk management process.

When one analyzes a project with the Gizmo, you shift the information curve (see Figure 7.1) and better understand the project and its risks. You improve your ability to address risks and opportunities sooner rather than later, resulting in a leaner project. Shifting the information curve with the Gizmo can improve project success probability and deliver value meeting users' expectations.

---

[1] The Project Management Gizmo is used with permission from the International Project Management Association.

Table A2.1 Gizmo complexity attributes

Complexity attributes	Simple	Rating	Complex
1. Constraints	Few constraints	1 2 3 4 N/A	Numerous interdependent constraints
i. Human resources	Competent and available	1 2 3 4 N/A	Skills are lacking and/or unavailable
ii. Time/schedule	Ample time allowed, straightforward network	1 2 3 4 N/A	Challenged and complex interdependencies
iii. Budget/financing	Liberal with sufficient contingency	1 2 3 4 N/A	Challenged and/or inadequate
2. Relative project size	Small and easily managed	1 2 3 4 N/A	Extremely large
3. Project criticality	Low criticality	1 2 3 4 N/A	Extreme criticality
i. Importance	Minor importance to organization	1 2 3 4 N/A	Extremely important to organization
ii. Priority	Low priority	1 2 3 4 N/A	Top priority
iii. Impact	Failure results in no long-term impacts	1 2 3 4 N/A	Project fails, organization fails
4. Uncertainty and risk	Risks and possible outcomes are identified	1 2 3 4 N/A	Copious risks with broad possible outcomes
5. Organizational environment	Project management friendly and mature	1 2 3 4 N/A	Project management hostile and immature
i. Culture	Homogeneous and peaceful	1 2 3 4 N/A	Diverse with conflict
ii. Governance	Simple, clear lines of responsibility	1 2 3 4 N/A	Complex, multiple companies, conflict
6. Business environment	Project friendly	1 2 3 4 N/A	Challenging, difficult, complex, arbitrary
i. Governance	Fair, open, predictable	1 2 3 4 N/A	Unjust, unpredictable, corruptible
ii. Economy	Stable, healthy	1 2 3 4 N/A	Volatile, weak
iii. Language	Homogeneous	1 2 3 4 N/A	Heterogeneous
iv. Political climate	Fair, open, predictable	1 2 3 4 N/A	Unjust, unpredictable, corruptible

Complexity attribute description	
1. Constraints: Things that get in the way of carrying out project tasks 1.1. Human resources: The people may not have the skills and/or be unavailable when needed 1.2. Time/schedule: The amount of time may or may not be enough to complete the project based on the approved durations 1.3. Budget/financing: There may or may not be enough resources to complete the approved scope of the work **2. Relative project size**: Projects become more complex as size increases; however, size is relative to the experience and capabilities of the organization. The impacts and probability of occurrence of risk events external to the project for successfully completing the project vary from low to extreme **3. Project criticality**: The degree the project affects the viability and operational future of the organizations involved 3.1. Importance: How significant the project is to an organization's strategy 3.2. Priority: The project's preference when another "competing" project is presented for managerial decision and action 3.3. Impact: The effect a successful or unsuccessful project will have on the organizations and stakeholders involved	**4. Uncertainty and risk**: Risk is something that leads to a change in outcomes, while uncertainty is the range of possible outcomes. Here, we assess the risks and uncertainty of the environment external to the project work itself **5. Organizational environment**: The setting(s) that the project will be planned and managed 5.1. Culture: The degree the culture (customs, traditions, speech, rituals, dress, manners, etc.) of the organization is aligned with the project's objectives, tools, and processes 5.2. Governance: The degree the organization oversees its operations is compatible with how those in the project want to plan and manage **6. Business environment**: The degree the business environment facilitates project completion 6.1. Culture: The degree the culture (customs, traditions, etc.) external to the organization is aligned with the project's objectives, tools, and processes 6.2. Governance: The degree the way the municipality/city/country is compatible with the way those in the project want to plan and manage 6.3. Economy: The degree the economy(ies) facilitate project completion 6.4. Language: The degree that the language used in the business setting is understood by those in the project 6.5. Political climate: The degree of stability of the political situation

Table A2.2 Gizmo effort attributes

Effort attributes	Simple	Rating	Complex
1. Type of work	Routine, simple, uncomplicated	1 2 3 4 N/A	Complicated, unpredictable, dangerous
1.1 Technology	Simple, proven, reliable	1 2 3 4 N/A	Complicated, novel, unreliable
1.2 Required competencies	Low skilled, abundant	1 2 3 4 N/A	Highly skilled, unavailable
1.3 Attractiveness	Desirable and sought after	1 2 3 4 N/A	Unpleasant, shunned
1.4 Uniqueness	Routine, typical	1 2 3 4 N/A	Exceptional, rare
2. Communications	Easy, effective, enjoyable	1 2 3 4 N/A	Hostile, difficult, complex, confusion
2.1 Number of stakeholders	Few	1 2 3 4 N/A	Numerous
2.2 Geographic dispersion	Close by (same building or city)	1 2 3 4 N/A	Scattered (different countries)
3. Integration scope	Aligned, simple, cohesive	1 2 3 4 N/A	Division, confusion, vagueness
3.1 Number of interfaces	Few, simple, regular	1 2 3 4 N/A	Numerous, complex, ad hoc
3.2 Number of contracts	Few, well known to each other	1 2 3 4 N/A	Numerous, new
4. Uncertainty and risk	Risks and possible outcomes are identified	1 2 3 4 N/A	Copious with wide possible outcomes
Effort attributes description			

1. **Type of work**: Related to the product the project will produce (e.g., implement a cybersecurity analytics application vs conducting a cybersecurity audit)
1.1. Technology: The degree the technology is developed, simple to use, and proven
1.2. Required competencies: The degree the competencies are required is available
1.3. Attractiveness: The degree project stakeholders want to be involved with the project
1.4. Uniqueness: The degree the product and/or project has been done before
2. **Communications**: The ease of which open communications are effectively and efficiently planned, executed, and received
2.1. Number of stakeholders: The number of people the project team needs to communicate with
Geographic dispersion: The degree of stakeholder dispersal throughout the region, country, or world

3. **Integration scope**: The ease of managing the various project management activities and processes to produce the project's product
3.1. Number of interfaces: The number and difficulty of project elements that need coordination
3.2. Number of contracts: The number and complexity of contracts that need to be managed
4. **Uncertainty and risk**: Risk is something that leads to a change in outcomes, while uncertainty is the range of possible outcomes. The impacts and probability of occurrence of risk events for successfully completing the project vary from low to extreme

APPENDIX 3

Risk Register

The risk management process is reflected in the risk register and issue register. The risk register aligns with the risk management process: risk identification, analysis (qualitative), treatment, and monitoring and control (Table A3.1).

Table A3.1 Risk register

Heading	Description	Example
Risk ID	Each risk has a unique ID	R-144
Date entered	The date the risk is entered into the risk register	February 8, 2020 (write out the month to avoid confusion)
Entered by	The person who entered the risk. Always assign to a single person and never a team	Debbie Hart, Project Manager
Project	Project name	Big Data Lake
Phase	Project phase	Plan
Risk cause	The root cause of the risk	Due to manufacturing delays
Risk event	The risk that may affect your project	There is a risk the servers may arrive late
Risk effect	The consequence of the risk event	Resulting in a delay to the build phase
Probability of occurring	The likelihood the risk may occur: high, medium, or low	Medium
Impact	The impact to the project if the risk occurs: high, medium, or low	High
Severity	Probability × Impact = Severity High = 3, medium = 2, and low = 1	$2 \times 3 = 6$
Risk prevention action	The actions to prevent the risk	Order servers that can be delivered on time

Table A3.1 (Continued)

Heading	Description	Example
Prevented by	The person responsible for preventing the risk	Barry Blanchard
Risk mitigation action	The person responsible for mitigating the risk	Change project logic to delay server configuration
Mitigated by	The person responsible for mitigating the risk	Barry Blanchard
Risk resolution date	The date the risk must be prevented, or the risk will become an issue	May 22, 2020
Risk status	The degree the risk is under control	Red: The risk cannot be prevented, and an issue is raised
Issue ID	The issue ID if the risk cannot be prevented	I-22
Comments	Information about preventing, mitigating, and closing the risk	Servers are 6 months behind production (February 22, 2020) Servers will be delivered late; confirmed with procurement (March 16, 2020)

Risk Narrative

The project requires three servers for big data-intensive computing. However, due to a global thrust toward digital transformation, a global chip shortage results in manufacturing delays. The project manager has raised a risk (R-144) and updated the risk register (Table A3.1). Our infrastructure SME (Barry Blanchard) is managing procurement and has investigated the availability of other models of servers, but none are available to meet our schedule. To mitigate, the team will bring forward future work such as developing the test strategy and plan and creating the T2P checklist, to make room to catch up with server configuration, testing, and build activities. The project manager closes the risk, updates the risk register, and converts the risk to an issue (I-22).

Issue Narrative

The project manager opens an issue (I-22) that there is an issue that the servers will arrive four months late, resulting in a delay to the build phase (Table A3.2). The procuring SME has spoken with the vendor, and there is high certainty that the servers will arrive on or before August 14, 2020. The project team has reviewed the schedule and will bring forward work such as working on the design, testing, and T2P documents to minimize the impact of the delay.

Table A3.2 Issue register

Heading	Description	Example
Issue ID	Each issue has a unique ID	I-22
Date entered	The date the issue is entered into the issue register	March 16, 2020
Entered by	The person who entered the issue	Debbie Hart, Project Manager
Project	Project name	Big Data Lake
Phase	Project phase	Plan
Issue cause	The root cause of the issue	Due to manufacturing delays
Issue event	The issue that affects your project	There is an issue the servers will arrive 4 months late
Issue effect	The consequence of the issue event	Resulting in a delay to the build phase
Impact	The impact to the project: high, medium, or low	High
Issue resolution	The actions to resolve the issue	None
Resolved by	The person responsible for resolving the issue	Barry Blanchard
Resolution date	The date the issue must be resolved	August 14, 2020
Issue status	The degree the issue is under control	Red: The issue cannot be resolved in time
Comments	Information about resolving and closing the issue	Servers are 6 months behind manufacturing targets, but the vendor has promised a delivery date of August 14, 2020, resulting in a 4-month delay to the project (April 2, 2020)

APPENDIX 4

Career Planning

Quality improvement is central in our frameworks and an integral component for continued success. Achieving quality improvement is more likely with a holistic approach: look for improvement opportunities throughout the Service Management System to optimize the value streams for our users (Limited, AXELOS 2019, 83–86). When one takes a holistic approach, the people involved in producing value can also benefit from assessing and developing their competencies. The cybersecurity professional can take a structured approach to improve their capabilities with career planning.

It takes three to five years to become "proficient" in a cybersecurity role (Oltsik 2020, 6). The cybersecurity professional will likely develop and maintain technical competence in areas immediately related to their role. While technical proficiency is being established, the cybersecurity professional can begin to plan holistically and develop business-related capabilities in leadership, communications, and business practices (Oltsik 2020, 17). Cybersecurity professionals can anticipate future business demands and develop capabilities in emerging technologies of interest to their industry. For example, business is expected to adopt process automation and advanced analytics widely; therefore, development in these areas will benefit cybersecurity professionals. Lean and Six Sigma techniques can improve processes and reduce statistical variations (Stanton, Gough, Ballardie, Bartam, Bamber, and Sohal 2014, 16) and can support process automation projects. There are multiple ways to undertake career planning; however, let's first look at sustainable careers that can guide career planning.

Sustainable Project-Oriented Career

We researched project-oriented sustainable careers and identified critical actions to improve career sustainability (Skulmoski et al. 2020, 11–12).

A sustainable career is one where the work continues at a sustainable pace, and there is balance in one's life. One moves from project to project without unplanned interruptions. Career sustainability is a broad concern ranging from boxers who face the inevitability of leaving the ring, or mothers who take a leave of absence from paid employment to raise a family, or lawyers who need to win cases to stay employed. Technology SMEs are challenged to stay current with emerging technologies and master an expanding palette of digital functionalities in their software systems. In the Gig Economy and 4th Industrial Revolution, we are increasingly project-oriented and move from project to project, and sometimes organization to organization.

We found that career sustainability depends on two contributors: networking and upskilling (Skulmoski et al. 2020, 76). Networking with other professionals helps people find new opportunities. Staying connected increases one's capabilities and opens opportunities; career sustainability is improved. Upskilling or expanding one's competencies is another career sustainability driver. We improve career sustainability as we learn the skills to meet emerging demands (AI collaboration with robotics). Therefore, forward-thinking cybersecurity professionals will invest time to plan and nurture their careers.

The technology and cybersecurity skills gap problem has been well studied since it is a perennial and perhaps a wicked problem. Cybersecurity professionals are fortunate that there are many pathways to remain competent such as pursuing technical certifications in technical platforms (e.g., Azure) or in a cybersecurity framework (e.g., CISSP). Unfortunately, part of the cybersecurity skills gap problem is related to poor career planning: "As this and past reports indicate, organizations and cybersecurity professionals are not looking at the profession strategically. There is a continuous lack of training, career development, and long-term planning. As a result, cybersecurity professionals often muddle through their careers with little direction, jumping from job to job and enhancing their skill sets on the fly rather than in any systematic way" (Oltsik 2020, 5). That is, many IT professionals do not take a strategic approach to career planning. Some visualize competence progression within the ITIL framework using the T-Career model (DuMoulin 2019, 7).

Planning the T-Career

One can envision career development over time if we look to the career progression of our IT colleagues. One develops skills into skill sets that can be illustrated as a shape across a maturity and capability spectrum (Figure A4.1, after Demirkan and Spohrer 2015, 13). The basic depiction of a T-shape professional has been modified in *Shields Up,* where the horizontal part of the T represents business skills and the vertical part represents technical skills. The new university cybersecurity graduate has a technical foundation required to join an IT department and joins with an I-shape skill set. With time, the new cybersecurity professional settles and continues to learn the technologies required to perform their role. They may formally add vendor-specific technical certifications such as the Cisco Certified Network Associate Security certification or certify in a technique such as the Certified Ethical Hacker. The I-shape skillset broadens as SMEs accumulate technical skills and certifications.

Some cybersecurity professionals add business-related skills by taking courses in effective communications, conflict resolution, emotional intelligence, budgeting, time management, and so on, depicted in forming a horizontal bar over the I-shape, transforming the shape into the T-shape. T-shape professionals have both technical and business skills and have expanded opportunities such as managerial roles; they can provide more value to their organizations and have improved career sustainability. Those who rise to chief information security officers (CISOs) have a

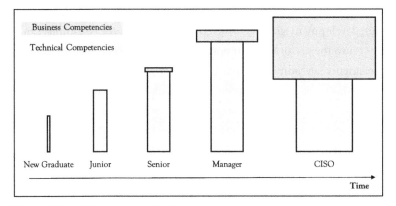

Figure A4.1 Competence development journey

foundation of technical skills, capped with a broad and deep business skill set. Conduct your job search for CISO positions, and you will find job requirements that emphasize the business skill set, such as:

1. Provide guidance to the CIO and the C-Suite leadership team and define and deliver strategic objectives while building goodwill and positive relationships.
2. Lead information security strategic planning and budgeting cycles supported with security and compliance targets, strategies, metrics, and reporting dashboards.
3. Create education and awareness programs that improve cybersecurity hygiene.

The CISO needs a foundation of technical skills with a greater emphasis on business skills to manage the entire ITIL Service Value System that includes projects and operations to deliver value for the organization. These three examples of CISO job requirements all involve project management: the foundation of delivering innovation, digital transformation, and sustained value. Therefore, understanding your career targets and the type of role you aspire to can help you with effective career planning.

Career Planning Process

If done correctly, career planning is a regular occurrence, such as during annual performance assessments so that your organization can support your development goals (Oltsik 2020, 6). Your career planning can be input into the performance appraisal. Some consider annual performance assessments an administrative burden; however, career planning can propel one's career with a strategic approach. Like project success, great careers do not happen by accident; great careers are planned, managed, and controlled. Career planning can be completed in three steps:

1. **Self-assessment:** Hiring managers use various "inventories" to assess capabilities and aptitudes in the new hire selection process. Many of these inventories are available to gain additional insight during career planning (e.g., search online for career and career planning

inventories for more formal self-assessment methods). These often can help identify strengths and areas to develop. Where are you in your competence development? Is your career development shape an I, or are you forming a T-shape career for balanced development (Figure A4.1)?

2. **Exploration:** Think about the type of position you would like in 5 to 10 years. Search online for job descriptions for those target positions to understand the ideal competency set. For example, if you aim to become a cybersecurity manager, search online for this position to understand better the types of experiences and competencies that people in these target positions possess.

3. **Career action plan:** Conduct a gap analysis between your competencies and your target job (e.g., cybersecurity manager) competencies. Then, develop a plan to acquire the related experience, knowledge, and skills.

Notice the similarity with cybersecurity maturity best practices? Complete a self-assessment, identify gaps, and develop an action plan to reach your targets. We follow this process in our organizations, and we can use it in our career planning.

Technical Competence Development

We are offered a wide array of career development opportunities, but we should be strategic: think about the skills needed today and in the future. Continue your technical development and add skills in emerging technologies such as collaborative AI, multimodal interfaces (e.g., seeing, hearing, and touching), and secure distributed ledgers (e.g., blockchain). Think about preparing for tomorrow's technical opportunities. Identify future technical skill shortages and begin learning about solutions such as machine learning. Create a plan to acquire these skills and knowledge; certifications are a natural pathway to technical competence. However, many certifications have a short-value period; some certifications can become obsolete as emerging technologies surpass the underlying technology. For example, Microsoft planned the retirement of MCSA, MCSD, and MCSE certifications as the cloud gains prominence and

Azure certifications emerge (Foley 2021, 1). The crux is that maintaining competence through technical certifications is a never-ending pursuit.

Nontechnical Competence Development

The pathway to senior IT roles is through a combination of technical and nontechnical excellence. When you search online for "what skills do CISOs need?" notice that the lists include very few technical skills! Most of the CISO skills are soft skills like effective communications, collaboration, and negotiation. Indeed, these are the types of skills robots lack! We discover that strategic planning and delivering innovation are frequently listed as essential skills; CISOs use project management tools and processes to bring strategy and other innovations to life. Therefore, your development journey through project management can bring you closer to the CISO and other senior roles.

Many nontechnical growth opportunities range from formal studies in a Master of Business Administration (MBA) degree to training and certification opportunities like Lean Six Sigma and project management certifications (Ottmann and Skulmoski 2020, 3). Certifications take less time to complete than university degrees and can fill in competencies gaps. The MBA degree is also variable where one can do a general MBA degree or an applied degree (e.g., MBA with Project Management Specialization or MBA in Innovation Management). Universities are improving their service value streams by offering many learning pathways like part-time studies, stackable degrees, and microcredentials to tailor learning to the individual student.

Approach your nontechnical training from a holistic perspective; think about the service value stream and how organizations approve projects to deliver innovations to the end user. Organizations follow the project management process and then hand over the product or service to operations to manage and optimize the service (Figure 1.1). Therefore, a well-rounded cybersecurity professional will have training and education in both the project and operations side. A project-oriented certification like the PMP or PRINCE with an MBA degree or Lean Six Sigma credential will help prepare oneself for leadership roles. Again, look at the competencies of managerial and leadership positions listed by recruiters to understand the desired/target skill set.

Undertaking career planning in conjunction with an annual performance review can better position you to not only score well on the assessment but help you stand out for your thoroughness. Few IT professionals look beyond a year or two in their career planning, and most have a narrow focus on technical competence development. You will stand out if you also include business skills like project management and Lean Six Sigma in your training plan. It is not uncommon for organizations to support high-value employees (e.g., cybersecurity professionals) and pay for MBA studies from top universities. Plan and ask for support! Organizations struggle to find and keep cybersecurity talent. Organizations can keep their best people by supporting career planning and providing financial support for training and education and secondments and appointments to other positions to gain broad experience.

With additional training, the cybersecurity professional gains new knowledge and skills; look for opportunities to apply these new competencies. You may work toward promotion within your organization to gain new experiences. However, a lateral transfer to a position such as Service Desk Queue Manager, IT Contracts Manager, and IT Service Quality Manager can also provide valuable growth experiences. These positions are within the technology department, but outside of cybersecurity; gaining experience in broad areas increases your understanding of the overall IT department and its services. You might also volunteer to "cover" for others when they take annual leave; you gain diverse experiences and accelerate your learning by covering for others. These lateral and coverage opportunities will expand your knowledge and skills in peripheral areas but also holistically.

Microlearning

Following are some useful exercises to enhance your learning:

- Look for articles about microlearning and continuous professional development to better understand this powerful mode of learning.
- Search online for the career planning process and use tailoring to follow a process that makes sense to you.

- Search job ads for senior technology positions to better understand emerging job requirements and associated competencies. Identify target competencies for development.
- Look for balance so that you are developing technical and nontechnical competencies like leadership, communication, and project management.
- Identify and develop lasting competencies (e.g., project management) that will not quickly become obsolete like many technical certifications becoming obsolete as new technologies emerge.

References

Aaldering, L.J., and C.H. Song. 2021. "Of Leaders and Laggards—Towards Digitalization of the Process Industries." *Technovation* 105, pp. 1–15. doi.10.1016/j.technovation.2020.102211

Aaser, M., and D. McElhaney. 2021. "Harnessing the Power of External Data." *McKinsey and Co.* www.mckinsey.com/business-functions/mckinsey-digital/our-insights/harnessing-the-power-of-external-data (accessed October 23, 2021).

AgileManifesto.org. 2001. "Manifesto for Agile Software Development." *AgileManifesto.org.* https://agilemanifesto.org/ (accessed October 17, 2019).

Allied Telesis. 2021. "Federal Government Solutions." *Allied Telesis.* www.alliedtelesis.com/au/en/solutions/industry/federal-government (accessed October 23, 2021).

AustCyber. 2020. "AustCyber Launches New Digital Trust Report Showing Jobs and Revenue at Stake." *AustCyber.* www.austcyber.com/news-events/austcyber-launches-new-digital-trust-report-showing-jobs-and-revenue-stake (accessed October 23, 2021).

Australian Government. 2021. "Strengthening Australia's Cyber Security Regulations and Incentives." *Australian Government Department of Home Affairs.* www.homeaffairs.gov.au/reports-and-publications/submissions-and-discussion-papers/cyber-security-regulations-incentives (accessed July 26, 2021).

Azanha, A., A.R.T.T. Argoud, J.B. de Camargo Junior, and P.D. Antoniolli. 2017. "Agile Project Management with Scrum." *International Journal of Managing Projects in Business* 10, no. 1, pp. 121–142. doi:10.1108/IJMPB-06-2016-0054

Barquin, S., R. Dreischmeier, S. Hertli, J. Königsfeld, and A. Roth. 2020. "The Big Boost: How Incumbents Successfully Scale their New Businesses." *McKinsey and Co.* www.mckinsey.com/business-functions/mckinsey-digital/our-insights/the-big-boost-how-incumbents-successfully-scale-their-new-businesses (accessed October 23, 2021).

Berger, D., N. Shashidhar, and C. Varol. June 1–2, 2020. "Using ITIL 4 in Security Management." *8th International Symposium on Digital Forensics and Security*, Beirut, Lebanon. doi:10.1109/ISDFS49300.2020.9116257

Bersin, J., and M. Zao-Sanders. 2019. "Making Learning a Part of Everyday Work." *Harvard Business Review.* https://hbr.org/2019/02/making-learning-a-part-of-everyday-work (accessed July 21, 2021).

Blackburn, S., L. LaBerge, C. O'Toole, and J. Schneider. 2020. "Digital Strategy in a Time of Crisis." *McKinsey and Co.* www.mckinsey.com/~/media/McKinsey/Business%20Functions/McKinsey%20Digital/Our%20Insights/Digital%20strategy%20in%20a%20time%20of%20crisis/Digital-strategy-in-a-time-of-crisis-final.pdf (accessed July 20, 2021).

Bleich, C. 2021. "The Top 11 Types of Microlearning for Your Employees." *Edgepoint Learning.* www.edgepointlearning.com/blog/types-of-microlearning/ (accessed July 19, 2021).

Boehm, J., and J. Smith. 2021. "Derisking Digital and Analytics Transformations." *McKinsey and Co.* www.mckinsey.com/business-functions/risk-and-resilience/our-insights/derisking-digital-and-analytics-transformations (accessed October 23, 2021).

Claus, I. 2017. "IT Security 2025: This is What Experts are Expecting for the Future." *Radar Services.* www.radarcs.com/wp-content/uploads/2020/04/IT-Security-Magazine-Issue-1-EN.pdf (accessed July 21, 2021).

Columbus, L. 2020. "The Best Cybersecurity Predictions for 2021 Roundup." *Forbes.* www.forbes.com/sites/louiscolumbus/2020/12/15/the-best-cybersecurity-predictions-for-2021-roundup/?sh=1bff550d5e8c (accessed July 21, 2021).

Corbo, J., and I. Ostojic. 2021. "The Top Trends in Tech." *McKinsey and Co.* www.mckinsey.com/business-functions/mckinsey-digital/our-insights/the-top-trends-in-tech (accessed July 12, 2021).

Creese, S., J. Saunders, L. Axon, and W. Dixon. 2020. "Future Series: Cybersecurity, Emerging Technology and Systemic Risk." *World Economic Forum.* www.weforum.org/reports/future-series-cybersecurity-emerging-technology-and-systemic-risk (accessed July 19, 2021).

CyberEdge Group, LLC. 2020. "2020 Cyberthreat Defense Report." *CyberEdge Group.* https://cybelangel.com/wp-content/uploads/2020/12/CyberEdge-2020-CDR-Report-v1.0-1.pdf (accessed July 7, 2021).

Dahlqvist, F., M. Patel, A. Rajko, and J. Shulman. 2019. "Growing Opportunities in the Internet of Things." *McKinsey and Co.* www.mckinsey.com/industries/private-equity-and-principal-investors/our-insights/growing-opportunities-in-the-internet-of-things (accessed October 23, 2021).

Daniel, H.Z., D.J. Hempel, and N. Srinivasan. 2003. "Project Selection: A Process Analysis." *Industrial Marketing Management* 32, no. 1, pp. 39–54. doi: 10.1016/S0019-8501(01)00193-6

Defossez, K., M. McMillan, and H. Vuppala. 2020. "Managing Large Technology Programs in the Digital Era." *McKinsey and Co.* www.mckinsey.com/business-functions/mckinsey-digital/our-insights/managing-large-technology-programs-in-the-digital-era (accessed July 20, 2021).

de Mast, J., and L. Lokkerbol. 2012. "An Analysis of the Six Sigma DMAIC Method from the Perspective of Problem Solving." *International Journal of Production Economics* 139, no. 2, pp. 604–614. doi:10.1016/j.ijpe.2012.05.035.

Demirkan, H., and J. Spohrer. 2015. "T-Shaped Innovators: Identifying the Right Talent to Support Service Innovation." *Research Technology Management* 58, no. 5, pp. 12–15. doi:10.5437/08956308X5805007

Dhasarathy, A., I. Gill, and N. Khan. 2020. "The CIO Challenge: Modern Business Needs a New Kind of Tech Leader." *McKinsey and Co.* www.mckinsey .com/business-functions/mckinsey-digital/our-insights/the-cio-challenge-modern-business-needs-a-new-kind-of-tech-leader?cid=other-eml-alt-mip-mck&hdpid=f911b6ba-0f2b-48df-8075-bde50f046eae&hctky=1178-6173&hlkid=8085fc1d99964a10b87a8b10c523781e (accessed July 31, 2021).

Diana, F., and S. Torrance. 2020. "Defining Your Digital Ecosystem: The First Step in a Machine First™ Transformation." *TATA Consultancy Services.* www .tcs.com/perspectives/articles/defining-your-digital-ecosystem-the-first-step-in-a-machine-first-transformation (accessed July 13, 2021).

Dietz, M., H. Khan, and I. Rab. 2020. "How do Companies Create Value from Digital Ecosystems?" *McKinsey and Co.* www.mckinsey.com/business-functions/mckinsey-digital/our-insights/how-do-companies-create-value-from-digital-ecosystems (Accessed October 23, 2021).

Drury, M., K. Conboy, and K. Power. 2012. "Obstacles to Decision Making in Agile Software Development Teams." *The Journal of Systems & Software* 85, no. 6, pp. 1239–1254. doi:10.1016/j.jss.2012.01.058

DuMoulin, T. 2019. "T-Shaped Professionals for a Digital Economy White Paper." *AXELOS.* www.axelos.com/resource-hub/white-paper/t-shaped-professionals-for-a-digital-economy (accessed July 20, 2021).

European Commission. 2021a. "Cybersecurity Policies." *European Commission.* https://digital-strategy.ec.europa.eu/en/policies/cybersecurity-policies#ecl-inpage-kmq7cvh2 (accessed July 26, 2021).

European Commission. 2021b. "The EU Cybersecurity Act." *European Commission.* https://digital-strategy.ec.europa.eu/en/policies/cybersecurity-act (accessed July 20, 2021).

Fitzpatrick, M., and K. Strovink. 2021. "How do You Measure Success in Digital? Five Metrics for CEOs." *McKinsey and Co.* www.mckinsey.com/business-functions/mckinsey-digital/our-insights/how-do-you-measure-success-in-digital-five-metrics-for-ceos (accessed October 23, 2021).

Foley, M.J. 2021. "Microsoft is Readying a New Windows Server Certification." *ZDNet.* www.zdnet.com/article/microsoft-is-readying-two-new-windows-server-certifications/ (accessed July 21, 2021).

Fox, J. 2021. "What is Cybersecurity Maturity Model Certification (CMMC)?" *Cobalt.* https://cobalt.io/blog/what-is-cybersecurity-maturity-model-certification-cmmc (accessed July 26, 2021).

Garba, A., M.B. Sirat, and S.J. Othman. 2020. "An Explanatory Review on Cybersecurity Capability Maturity Models." *Advances in Science, Technology and Engineering Systems Journal* 5, no. 4, pp. 762–769. doi:10.25046/aj050490

Gartner. 2020a. "The IT Roadmap for Cybersecurity." *Gartner*. www.gartner.com/en/information-technology/trends/the-it-roadmap-for-cybersecurity (accessed October 23, 2021).

Gartner. 2020b. "The 2021 CIO Agenda: Seize this Opportunity for Digital Business Acceleration." *Gartner*. www.gartner.com/en/documents/3991898/the-2021-cio-agenda-seize-this-opportunity-for-digital-b (accessed October 23, 2021).

Gemino, A., B. Horner Reich, and P.M. Serrador. 2021. "Agile, Traditional, and Hybrid Approaches to Project Success: Is Hybrid a Poor Second Choice?" *Project Management Journal* 52, no. 2, pp. 161–175. doi:10.1177/8756972820973082

George, J. March 3–5, 2008. "Significance of Technology Management and Project Management Aligned with Portfolio Management is Vital for Any Project Based Organisation." *PMI® Global Congress 2008—Asia Pacific*, Sydney, Australia. www.pmi.org/learning/library/technology-project-management-aligned-7144

Global Knowledge. 2021. "15 Top-Paying IT Certifications for 2021." *Global Knowledge*. www.globalknowledge.com/us-en/resources/resource-library/articles/top-paying-certifications/#gref (accessed October 24, 2021).

Göbel, H., and S. Cronholm. 2015. "ITIL Experiences: Benefits & Barriers." *DiVa*. www.diva-portal.org/smash/get/diva2:1338228/FULLTEXT01.pdf (accessed July 20, 2021).

Gonzalo, A., H. Harreis, C.S. Altable, and C. Villepelet. 2020. "Fashion's Digital Transformation: Now or Never." *McKinsey and Co.* www.mckinsey.com/industries/retail/our-insights/fashions-digital-transformation-now-or-never (accessed October 23, 2021).

Groombridge, D. 2021. "Gartner Top Strategic Technology Trends for 2022." *Gartner*. www.gartner.com/en/information-technology/insights/top-technology-trends?utm_campaign=RM_NA_2021_SWG_NL_17_IT&utm_medium=email&utm_source=Eloqua&cm_mmc=Eloqua-_-Email-_-LM_RM_NA_2021_SWG_NL_17_IT-_-0000 (accessed November 8, 2021).

Hale, R. 2017. "Cyber Competencies and the Cybersecurity Officer." In *The Cyber Risk Handbook*, ed. D. Antonucci, 358–368. Hoboken: John Wiley & Sons. doi:10.1002/9781119309741

Hartman, F.T. 1999a. *Ability to Change Paradox*. Presented in a Project Management Class, University of Calgary, Canada.

Hartman, F.T. 1999b. *PLOs*. Presented in a project management class, University of Calgary, Canada.

Horan, J. 2020. "The Current State of DOD's Cybersecurity Maturity Model Certification Program." *Contract Management* 60, no. 7, pp. 8–16. www .proquest.com/docview/2458774404?parentSessionId=LYs2%2F3upC AUd%2BawTyjPWYgQ%2BINRl9%2FDUtgirauOSFRo%3D&pq-origsite=primo&accountid=26503

Howard, C. 2020. "Top Priorities for IT: Leadership Vision for 2021." *Gartner*. www.gartner.com/en/publications/cio-top-priorities-leadership-vision-2021 (accessed July 19, 2021).

IBM. 2021. "Cleveland Clinic and IBM Unveil Landmark 10-Year Partnership to Accelerate Discovery in Healthcare and Life Sciences." *IBM*. https:// newsroom.ibm.com/2021-03-30-Cleveland-Clinic-and-IBM-Unveil-Landmark-10-Year-Partnership-to-Accelerate-Discovery-in-Healthcare-and-Life-Sciences (accessed October 07, 2021).

ISO. 2000. *ISO 9004:2000 Quality Management Systems—Guidelines for Performance Improvements*. ISO. www.iso.org/standard/28692.html (accessed July 21, 2021).

ISO. 2013a. *ISO/IEC 27001 Information Technology—Security Techniques—Information Security Management Systems—Requirements*. ISO. www.iso.org/ isoiec-27001-information-security.html (accessed October 07, 2021).

ISO. 2013b. *ISO/IEC 27002:2013 Code of Practice for Information Security Controls*. ISO. www.iso.org/standard/54533.html (accessed July 20, 2021).

ISO. 2018a. *ISO/IEC 27000:2018 Information Security Management Systems—Overview and Vocabulary*. ISO. www.iso.org/standard/73906.html (accessed July 20, 2021).

ISO 31000. 2018b. *Risk management—Guidelines*. ISO. www.iso.org/ standard/65694.html (accessed July 20, 2021).

Kerzner, H. 2013. *Project Management a Systems Approach to Planning, Scheduling, and Controlling*. 11th ed. Hoboken, N.J: John Wiley & Sons, Inc. www .wiley.com/en-au/Project+Management%3A+A+Systems+Approach+to+ Planning%2C+Scheduling%2C+and+Controlling%2C+11th+Edition-p-97 81118415856

Leal, R. 2015. "Achieving Continual Improvement through the use of Maturity Models." *Advisera Expert Solutions Ltd*. https://advisera.com/27001academy/ blog/2015/04/13/achieving-continual-improvement-through-the-use-of-maturity-models/ (accessed October 24, 2021).

Limited, AXELOS. 2019. *ITIL® Foundation: ITIL 4 Edition*. London: The Stationery Office Ltd, 2019. www.axelos.com/for-professionals/publications

Marks, J. June 11, 2021. "The Cybersecurity 202: Our Expert Network Says it's Time for More Cybersecurity Regulations." *The Washington Post*. www .washingtonpost.com/politics/2021/06/11/cybersecurity-202-our-expert-network-says-it-time-more-cybersecurity-regulations/ (accessed July 21, 2021).

Marrone, M., M. Kiessling, and L.M. Kolbe. June 02–05, 2010. "Are we really Innovating? An Exploratory Study on Innovation Management and Service Management." *2010 IEEE International Conference on Management of Innovation & Technology.* Singapore. doi:10.1109/ICMIT.2010.5492719

Marrone, M., and L.M. Kolbe. 2011. "Uncovering ITIL Claims: IT Executives' Perception on Benefits and Business-IT Alignment." *Information Systems and E-Business Management* 9, no. 3, pp. 381–382. doi:10.1007/s10257-010-0163-z

Maurer, T., and A. Nelson. 2020. "International Strategy to Better Protect the Financial System Against Cyber Threats." *Carnegie Endowment for International Peace.* https://carnegieendowment.org/2020/11/18/international-strategy-to-better-protect-financial-system-against-cyber-threats-pub-83105 (accessed July 20, 2021).

McHugh, B. 2020. "Gartner's IT Automation Predictions for 2021." *Advanced Systems Concepts.* www.advsyscon.com/blog/gartner-it-automation/ (accessed July 20, 2021).

Microsoft. 2020. "Microsoft Digital Defense Report." *Microsoft.* www.microsoft.com/en-us/download/details.aspx?id=101738 (accessed July 7, 2021).

Morgan, S. 2019. "The 2019\2020 Official Annual Cybersecurity Jobs Report." *Herjavec Group.* www.herjavecgroup.com/2019-cybersecurity-jobs-report-cybersecurity-ventures/ (accessed July 21, 2021).

Moyer, K. 2021. "The C-Suite Guide: Accelerate Digital for Future-Ready Business." *McKinsey and Co.* www.gartner.com/en/insights/sustain-your-digital-momentum (accessed July 21, 2021).

MuleSoft. 2020. "Top 7 Digital Transformation Trends Shaping 2020." *Mulesoft.* https://blogs.mulesoft.com/digital-transformation/digital-transformation-trends-shaping-2020/ (accessed October 23, 2021).

MuleSoft. 2021. "Top 8 Digital Transformation Trends Shaping 2021." *Mulesoft.* www.mulesoft.com/lp/reports/top-digital-transformation-trends-2021 (accessed October 23, 2021).

National Institute of Standards and Technology. 2018. *Framework for Improving Critical Infrastructure Cybersecurity.* 1st ed. doi.org/10.6028/NIST.CSWP .04162018

Obwegeser, N., T. Yokoi, M. Wade, and T. Voskes. 2020. "7 Key Principles to Govern Digital Initiatives." *MIT Sloan Management Review* 61, no. 3, pp. 1–9. https://ezproxy.bond.edu.au/login?url=https://www.proquest.com/scholarly-journals/7-key-principles-govern-digital-initiatives/docview/2405312501/se-2?accountid=26503

Oltsik, J. 2020. "ESG Research Report: The Life and Times of Cybersecurity Professionals 2020." *ESG.* www.esg-global.com/research/esg-research-report-the-life-and-times-of-cybersecurity-professionals-2020 (accessed July 21, 2021).

Ottmann, D., and G.J. Skulmoski. November 22–24, 2020. "Rapid and Responsive Sustainable Careers." *Rapid Cities—Responsive Architectures.* Dubai, United Arab Emirates. http://architecturemps.com/wp-content/uploads/2021/06/Amps-Proceedings-Series-21.pdf (accessed July 20, 2021).

Payette, J., E. Anegbe, E. Caceres, and S. Muegge. 2015. "Secure by Design: Cybersecurity Extensions to Project Management Maturity Models for Critical Infrastructure Projects." *Technology Innovation Management Review* 5, no. 6, pp. 26–34. doi:10.22215/timreview/904

Peacock, J. 2020. "2021 Predictions: Cyber Risk, Global Attacks, and Regulatory Change." *Security Boulevard.* https://securityboulevard.com/2020/12/2021-predictions-cyber-risk-global-attacks-and-regulatory-change/ (accessed July 20, 2021).

Pipikaite, A., M. Barrachin, and S. Crawford. 2021. "These are the Top Cybersecurity Challenges of 2021." *World Economic Forum.* www.weforum.org/agenda/2021/01/top-cybersecurity-challenges-of-2021/ (accessed July 28, 2021).

PMI. 1996. *A Guide to the Project Management Body of Knowledge (PMBOK Guide).* Newtown Square, Pennsylvania: Project Management Institute, Inc.

PMI. 2017a. *A Guide to the Project Management Body of Knowledge (PMBOK Guide).* Newtown Square, Pennsylvania: Project Management Institute, Inc. https://ebookcentral.proquest.com/lib/bond/detail.action?docID=5180849

PMI. 2017b. "Job Growth and Talent Gap: 2017-2027." *Project Management Institute.* www.pmi.org/learning/careers/job-growth (accessed July 21, 2021).

PMI. 2018. "The Project Manager of the Future: Developing Digital-Age Project Management Skills to Thrive in Disruptive Times." *Project Management Institute.* www.pmi.org/learning/thought-leadership/pulse/the-project-manager-of-the-future (accessed July 28, 2021).

PMI. 2019. "AI Innovators: Cracking the Code on Project Performance." *Project Management Institute.* www.pmi.org/learning/thought-leadership/pulse/ai-innovators (accessed July 21, 2021).

PMI. 2020. "The Innovation Imperative." *Project Management Institute.* www.pmi.org/learning/thought-leadership/pulse/the-innovation-imperative (accessed October 23, 2021).

PMI. 2021. *A Guide to the Project Management Body of Knowledge: PMBOK G uide.* 7th ed. Newtown Square, Pennsylvania: Project Management Institute, Inc. https://ebookcentral.proquest.com/lib/bond/detail.action?docID=6636132

PRINCE2.com. 2021. "What is PRINCE2?" *PRINCE2.com.* www.prince2.com/aus/what-is-prince2#:~:text=PRINCE2%20is%20a%20process%2Dbased,recognised%20all%20over%20the%20world (accessed July 21, 2021).

Ramakrishnan, A. 2014. "Benefits of Adopting Information Technology Infrastructure Library (ITIL): Gap Analysis of State of Academic Research and Practitioner Needs." *Journal of Management Research* 14, no. 3, pp. 159–168. www.proquest.com/scholarly-journals/benefits-adopting-information-technology/docview/2473444947/se-2?accountid=26503

Rea-Guaman, A.M., T. San Feliu, J.A. Calvo-Manzano, and I.D. Sanchez-Garcia. October 04–05, 2017. "Comparative Study of Cybersecurity Capability Maturity Models." *International Conference on Software Process Improvement and Capability Determination.* Springer, Palma de Mallorca, Spain. Accessed July 21, 2021. doi: 10.1007/978-3-319-67383-7_8

Rushe, D., and J. Borger. June 14, 2021. "Age of the Cyber-Attack: US Struggles to Curb Rise of Digital Destabilization." *The Guardian.* www.theguardian.com/technology/2021/jun/14/age-of-the-cyber-attack-us-digital-destabilization

Scheibenreif, D., and M. Raskino. 2021. "Machine Customers Will Decide Who Gets their Trillion-Dollar Business." *Gartner.* www.gartner.com/en/documents/4001543/machine-customers-will-decide-who-gets-their-trillion-do (accessed October 23, 2021).

Scholtz, T. 2021. "Rethink the Security and Risk Strategy." *Gartner.* www.gartner.com/en/publications/rethink-security-risk-strategy-ebook (accessed July 19, 2021).

Schwab, K. 2016. "The Fourth Industrial Revolution: What it Means, How to Respond." *World Economic Forum.* www.weforum.org/agenda/2016/01/the-fourth-industrial-revolution-what-it-means-and-how-to-respond/ (accessed July 20, 2021).

Schwaber K., and J. Sutherland. 2017. "The Scrum Guide™." *Scrum Guides.* https://scrumguides.org/ (accessed July 20, 2021).

Schwartz, M. 2019. "Government Agencies Field More Cybersecurity Maturity Models." *Information Security Media Group, Corp.* www.bankinfosecurity.com/government-agencies-field-more-capability-maturity-models-a-13071 (accessed July 26, 2021).

Sekgweleo, T. 2015. "Understanding Traditional Systems Development Methodologies." *International Journal of Advances in Management and Economics* 4, no. 3, pp. 51–58. www.managementjournal.info/index.php/IJAME/article/download/370/313 (accessed July 21, 2021).

Serrador, P., and J.K. Pinto. 2015. "Does Agile Work?—A Quantitative Analysis of Agile Project Success." *International Journal of Project Management* 33, no. 5, pp. 1040–1051. doi:10.1016/j.ijproman.2015.01.006

Skilton, M., and F. Hovsepian. 2018. *The 4th Industrial Revolution Responding to the Impact of Artificial Intelligence on Business,* 1st ed. Cham: Springer International Publishing. doi.org/10.1007/978-3-319-62479-2

Skulmoski, G.J., and F.T. Hartman. 2000. "The Project's Achilles Heel: Misalignment." *Cost Engineering* 42, no. 12, pp. 33–37. www.proquest

.com/docview/220443814?pq-origsite=gscholar&fromopenview=true (accessed July 19, 2021).

Skulmoski, G.J. November 09–11, 2008. "Project Selection Aided by the Project Feasibility Gizmo." *International Project Management Association World Congress*. Rome, Italy. www.ipma.world/pm-and-ipma-world-congress-in-italy-by-luigi-iperti/ (accessed July 20, 2021).

Skulmoski, G.J., C. Langston, A. Patching, and A. Ghanbaripour. 2020. "Sustainable Project-Oriented Careers: A Conceptual Model." In *Research on Project, Programme and Portfolio Management Integrating Sustainability into Project Management*, ed. R. Cuevas, C. Bodea, and P. Torres-Lima. New York, NY: Springer International Publishing. https://link.springer.com/book/10.1007/978-3-030-60139-3

Skulmoski, G., and F.S.A. Brendolan. 2022. "Hybrid Project Management in Post-Secondary Research and Education." In *Industry Practices, Processes and Techniques Adopted in Education*, eds. K. MacCallum and D. Parsons. Singapore: Springer.

Sliep, C., and C. Marnewick. 2020. "The Quest in Delivering Quality IT Services: The Case of a Higher Education Institution." *Education and Information Technologies* 25, no. 6, pp. 4817–4844. doi:10.1007/s10639-020-10198-0

Snee, R.D. 2010. "Lean Six Sigma—Getting Better all the Time." *International Journal of Lean Six Sigma* 1, no. 1, pp. 9–29. doi:10.1108/20401461011033130

Stanton, P., R. Gough, R. Ballardie, T. Bartram, G.J. Bamber, and A. Sohal. 2014. "Implementing Lean Management/Six Sigma in Hospitals: Beyond Empowerment or Work Intensification?" *International Journal of Human Resource Management* 25, no. 21, pp. 2926–2940. doi:10.1080/09585192.2014.963138

Tsunoda, H., and Y. Kino. 2018. "Evaluation of Detailed CSFs and Benefits Model for ITIL Implementation." *International Journal of Innovation, Management and Technology* 9, no. 4, pp. 145–151. doi:10.18178/ijimt.2018.9.4.804

Tucker, P. 2020. "More Industry Regulations are Needed to Improve US Cybersecurity, Congressional Report Says." *Defense One*. www.defenseone.com/technology/2020/03/more-industry-regulations-are-needed-improve-us-cybersecurity-congressional-report-says/163697/ (accessed July 26, 2021).

US Department of Energy. 2021. "Cybersecurity Capability Maturity Model." *US Department of Energy*. www.energy.gov/ceser/cybersecurity-capability-maturity-model-c2m2 (accessed July 26, 2021).

Warsinske, J., M. Graff, K.M. Henry, C. Hoover, B. Malisow, S. Murphy, C. Oakes, G. Pajari, J.T. Parker, D. Seidl, and M. Vasquez. 2019. *The Official (ISC)2 CISSP CBK Reference*. 5th ed. Newark: John Wiley & Sons, Incorporated. https://ebookcentral.proquest.com/lib/bond/detail.action?docID=5747370

The White House. 2021. "Executive Order on Improving the Nation's Cybersecurity." *The White House*. www.whitehouse.gov/briefing-room/

presidential-actions/2021/05/12/executive-order-on-improving-the-nations-cybersecurity/ (accessed October 23, 2021).

Williams, E., J. Galvin, and L. LaBerge. 2021. "The New Digital Edge: Rethinking Strategy for the Post-pandemic Era." *McKinsey and Co.* www.mckinsey.com/business-functions/mckinsey-digital/our-insights/the-new-digital-edge-rethinking-strategy-for-the-postpandemic-era (accessed July 21, 2021).

World Economic Forum. 2020. "Digital Transformation: Powering the Great Reset." *World Economic Forum.* www3.weforum.org/docs/WEF_Digital_Transformation_Powering_the_Great_Reset_2020.pdf (accessed July 26, 2021).

Zaydi, M., and B. Nassereddine. 2020. "DevSecOps Practices for an Agile and Secure IT Service Management." *Academy of Information and Management Sciences Journal* 23, no. 2, pp. 1–16. https://ezproxy.bond.edu.au/login?url=https://www.proquest.com/scholarly-journals/devsecops-practices-agile-secure-service/docview/2424965737/se-2?accountid=26503

About the Author

Gregory J. Skulmoski, BEd, MBA, PhD, CITP, FBCS, is a seasoned (and bruised!) project manager who has led technical and nontechnical projects in Australia, the Middle East, and Canada, with about $10 billion project experience. He is a Certified Information Technology Professional and a lifetime Fellow of the British Computer Society. Greg has a PhD in project management, where he focused his research on the competencies required for transformation and optimization projects. As a PhD student, he won the prestigious Robert J. Yourzak Scholarship Award from the Project Management Institute (PMI). Greg was a core member of PMI's the Guide to the Project Management Body of Knowledge® 2000 Update Team that revised the original PMI PMBOK® Guide (PMI 1996). He has contributed to other standards such as PMI's Practice Standard for Work Breakdown Structures, the Organizational Project Management Maturity Model, and the Project Manager Competency Development Framework. Greg has presented his research to technical audiences in over 16 countries, and his research has appeared in top-tier journals and books.

Dr. Skulmoski currently teaches project innovation management at Bond University in the Faculty of Society and Design. Greg's teaching focus is on practical processes and tools to successfully implement technology projects. Greg used these hybrid project management tools and processes to win the Chief Information Security Officers 2017 Middle East Security Award (for risk management in projects). Dr. Skulmoski is bringing theory and practice together in his book *Shields Up: Cybersecurity Project Management* for Business Experts Press (Due 2022). Greg plays drums, scuba dives, and likes to be outside with his family and friends.

Index

Concise and Applied Business Books

The Collection listed above is one of 30 business subject collections that Business Expert Press has grown to make BEP a premiere publisher of print and digital books. Our concise and applied books are for...

- Professionals and Practitioners
- Faculty who adopt our books for courses
- Librarians who know that BEP's Digital Libraries are a unique way to offer students ebooks to download, not restricted with any digital rights management
- Executive Training Course Leaders
- Business Seminar Organizers

Business Expert Press books are for anyone who needs to dig deeper on business ideas, goals, and solutions to everyday problems. Whether one print book, one ebook, or buying a digital library of 110 ebooks, we remain the affordable and smart way to be business smart. For more information, please visit www.businessexpertpress.com, or contact sales@businessexpertpress.com.

Made in United States
North Haven, CT
11 October 2023

42646748R00114